Unveiling the Truth:

Transforming Childhood Trauma

By

Laurie Jacobvitz

Unveiling the Truth: Transforming Childhood Trauma
Laurie Jacobvitz

Human Created Symbol of Distinction

ISBN 979-8-234-04021-3

For Little Laurie
And the inner child in all of us

The truth about our childhood is stored up in our body,
And although we can repress it, we can never alter it.
Our intellect can be deceived, our feelings manipulated,
Our perceptions confused,
And our body tricked with medication.
But someday our body will present its bill,
For it is as incorruptible as a child
Who, still whole in spirit,
Will accept no compromises or excuses,
And it will not stop tormenting us
Until we stop evading the truth.

—Alice Miller
Thou Shalt Not Be Aware: Society's Betrayal of the Child

Disclaimer:

The stories in this book reflect the author's recollection of events. Some names, locations and identifying characteristics have been changed to protect the privacy of those depicted. Dialogue has been re-created from memory.

Content Warning:

This book contains content about sexual abuse that may be disturbing for some readers. While the elements are handled with care and are essential to the narrative, this may be difficult for some to engage in fully. Take care of yourself and step away or skip sections if you need to.

Contents

Preface

In the summer of 2021, after I had just finished the first draft of my memoir, I received a phone call from my brother Ben. He said he had been looking through some boxes he had of Mom's things that he received after her passing and had found a memoir she had written called *Fractured, I Grow Stronger.* The main character in the memoir, he said, was me. He told me he would send me a copy.

The memoir was only 25 pages long but there were some shocking revelations of family secrets. After taking some time to process the information, I decided to integrate Mom's memoir with mine to show her perspective.

After each chapter, there is either an excerpt from her memoir or some of her poetry. Mom's words are printed in italics to distinguish them from mine. To further clarify, since her name was Marilyn Probe, I have added the word *Marilyn* before each excerpt along with the approximate year in which the event takes place.

Prologue

My safe place was in the corner of my bedroom. That is where I sat now in the middle of the night, my small body on the floor hugging my knees against my chest. I breathed a sigh of relief as I felt the walls holding me close. I squeezed my eyes shut and pressed my body hard into the crease where the walls met. I saw myself getting smaller and smaller wanting to disappear into the corner never to return. For a moment, time stood still. But when I opened my eyes, I was still there.

I was 5 years old in 1960 and very scared. I was not scared of dying. I was scared of Dad. I wanted to die because of Dad. I never knew what would happen when he was alone with me. The terror of what could happen next was just as awful as what he did to me. I didn't have names for the things he did, but I knew it lacerated my heart and scarred my body. I wanted to escape but I didn't know how.

On this sweltering July night in St. Louis, I climbed back into my bed discouraged and exhausted. My body felt way too hot and the bumps from the chicken pox were itching and oozing pus. Mom walked into the room, her full turquoise skirt rustling and her metal belt shining in the moonlight. I wanted to reach out and touch it to cool my skin, but I did not.

"Come on downstairs," she whispered so as not to wake my sister who slept in the bed next to me.

She had set up a cot on the screened-in back porch and it was a bit cooler than upstairs, but not much. She brought me a cold, wet cloth to put on my forehead.

Once Mom left, I lay in the dark hoping Dad stayed upstairs. I tried to disappear again, closing my eyes and pleading for the umpteenth time for something or someone to come take me away.

When I opened my eyes, I was surrounded by angels. A glowing white light enveloped me on my small, narrow cot and illuminated the entire porch. Engulfed in the light, I was in awe of its beauty and power.

One angel stood out from the others. She had alabaster skin and golden hair streaming out behind her. Fluttering aqua blue gauze surrounded her and huge white wings perched upon her back. I sat up and held out my arms in delight, thrilled someone had finally heard my plea.

"My name is Mariah," she said. "I am your guardian angel. It is not time yet for you to come with me."

"But I want to leave!" I protested. " I don't like it here. Please take me with you!"

"I'm sorry. I can't do that," she said apologetically.

"I don't care. I want to go. Please!" I begged with tears running down my cheeks.

"I can't explain to you why you can't go with me. You have to trust me. You must stay here."

"You are a mean angel," I said pouting.

"I love you. We all love you. You are so loved." She smiled at me, and I was unexpectedly filled with a sense of bliss sinking back onto the bed.

"Will I see you again?" I asked hopefully.

"Not for a long time because I'm going to help you forget and if you remember me, you will remember what happened to you." Mariah said.

"But I promise we will meet again when the time is right. I love you Laurie," she said, and her eyes held mine. Then she kissed me on the forehead and as quickly as they appeared, she and the other angels were gone.

Later when Mom came to check on me, my fever had soared. She called the ambulance to whisk me away into the unbearably hot night.

Marilyn

1961

The reason I went to Webster College to obtain my teaching certificate was because I was outraged at the way my daughter had been treated in first grade. Laurie, at six, was placed in the "slow" track with behaviorally disordered children. Laurie had fluffy strawberry blonde curls, was the tallest student in her class and walked awkwardly belying her beauty. The braces that the orthopedic surgeon directed me to put on her legs at 18 months had done nothing to correct the inward bent of her legs. Her favorite friends were our neighbors Joey and Grant, who fought over her in preschool and Wanda who lived two doors down.

"You say she did well on the reading readiness test, then why did you put her in the slow class?" I had asked.

"Well, it is true she did well, but she needed to try very hard to do that."

This was the conversation I had with the kindergarten teacher when Laurie was six after she had been two months in the "slow" first grade class. The kindergarten teacher's explanation never made sense to me. I would not know until years later that school was not the problem. It was our home.

Chapter One

The Angels Return

It was cold and dark in our tri-level track home when I walked down the carpeted stairs to get on the exercise bike. My husband Michael came down next to start the coffee maker and then went back up to read the newspaper in bed. After I finished on the bike, I dashed up the stairs and heard my son Noah in the shower. My daughter Rachel sleepily said "I'm up" when I knocked on her door. It was the year 2000 and we had all survived Y2K.

The sun was just peeking over the mountains in our suburban neighborhood in northern California. Rachel was not interested in eating anything for breakfast and Noah grabbed some toast and fruit. Michael was off to commute to his engineering firm. I hurried so I could drop off Rachel at the local elementary school and Noah and I could arrive at the middle school before the bell. It was always a last-minute dash to make it on time.

My life was run by the bells of school. About a one-hour drive north of San Francisco, the middle school was open air style with cheap modular units dotting the concrete. Noah ran to class, and I ran down the hall to the room with my deaf student squeezing into my folding chair just as the bell rang. The teacher was a thin, wiry man with bright red hair and a contagious smile. He started scribbling the math problems on the board for the day's lesson and I raised my hands to start signing.

"A variable," he said "is actually a letter that stands for a number..."

"2x = 4. How do you solve this? You want to get the letter x by itself. Divide 2x by 2 and whatever you do to one side of the equation, you must do to the other side."

I felt a familiar wave of anger and grief sweep over me unexpectedly taking my breath away. I wanted to run out of the room, but that was not possible, so I took deep breaths to keep my equilibrium. When the bell rang, I went into the bathroom and splashed water on my face. What was going on? What were these emotions trying to tell me? Could I be this upset about Noah's Bar Mitzvah preparations or dealing with our Amway business? It felt like more than that.

When I got home that afternoon, I was inundated with phone calls from other Amway distributors.

"I have a customer and they didn't get their products," the woman on the phone said. "What do I do?"

I looked up at the clock when the phone stopped ringing. It was 5 pm and I needed to get dinner ready. Michael had to eat dinner quickly, get dressed in his suit and tie, and then go out to show the Amway business plan. I felt like Atlas holding the world on his shoulders. Maybe I was just too busy and that is why I had waves of intense emotions pouring through me at inopportune times.

The wave struck again. I hung onto the kitchen counter for support. Fear ran through me like electrical impulses on a live wire. "Mom," said Noah coming into the kitchen. "I'm hungry. Can I have something to eat?"

"You can wait an hour," I said irritated. "We'll be eating soon."

"But I'm hungry now," he insisted.

"If you eat now, you won't be hungry for dinner. I'm working as fast as I can," I said dismissively.

"What are we having?" he asked.

"Chicken, rice and broccoli," I said.

"Chicken, chicken, chicken—we always have chicken," he said with a pout.

"Go upstairs," I said at my wits end. "I will tell you when dinner is ready."

He left in a huff. My stomach was twisting in pain. When Michael finally came home from work, I went up to our bedroom to talk to him.

"Something is wrong," I said. Anger, grief and shame are overwhelming me and I'm having a hard time coping. I need to find out what's going on. I heard about this psychic healer, and I want to see if she can help me."

"Ok," he said hurriedly putting on his suit. "If you think it will help, that's fine with me."

I scheduled a psychic healing with a woman named Mabel for the following week. She set up a massage table in the small office on the ground floor of our home. As soon as she put her hands on me, I was surrounded by this powerful white light that pierced my heart with goodness. I felt a suffusion of peace unlike anything I'd ever experienced. Angels were singing and the sound they made was entrancing and held me spellbound. They appeared as glowing orbs enveloped with a translucent material that flowed behind them in curling waves.

As I relaxed on the massage table, Mabel led me in a visualization to go back into my childhood.

I was sitting in the corner of my bedroom trying to disappear. I hugged my knees and wished to get smaller and smaller like

Alice in Wonderland, but when I opened my eyes, I was still there. I was so scared that my heart was pounding in my chest, and I could hardly breathe.

The image was so familiar, so visceral that I felt tears coming down my cheeks. I hadn't thought about that little girl in so long. She was reaching out to me, and I needed to listen.

After the healing, my body felt completely different; the vestiges of peace and the energy of the angels were still with me. I sat on our raggedy green futon with Mabel in that space between waking and sleeping.

"I'm not sure what that vision meant," I said groggily.

"It was your father," she said gently. "You're a victim of sexual abuse."

A sharp pain struck me as she spoke. It ripped away the peace, ravaging through my stomach and intestines like water crashing through a dike. I doubled over. Mabel had me lie down.

"I don't believe you. I don't think my father would do something like that," I mumbled.

"It is hard to face," she said, her eyes full of compassion.

"No!" I said. "That's not possible. I would have remembered that." She looked at me with sorrow in her eyes.

"I don't believe you!" I yelled. She did not try to convince me. I paid her and she left.

I was bereft and filled with enormous angst and fear. I knew something happened in my past that was trying to come through, but I never would have guessed sexual abuse. I was in shock.

Afterwards, I approached Michael as he was reading a book in our bedroom.

"I had the psychic healing today with Mabel," I said. "I think something happened with Dad when I was young. During my healing, I got an image of me as a young girl, terrified."

"What did you see?" he asked as he put the book down.

"I saw myself at about 5 years old sitting in a corner in my bedroom trying to disappear and go back where I came from. Then Mabel told me that I had been sexually abused by my father as a young girl."

He was quiet for a moment. "Do you think she's right?"

"I don't know," I whispered, my head hanging down. "I just don't know."

"Oh Laurie," he said and took me in his arms. We lay there for a while. I wanted to cry but couldn't. I was still stunned. He reassured me and comforted me. Then he asked me again if I thought it was true.

"Possibly," I ventured.

"I've never liked your Dad," he said angrily in a low voice. "He takes over the room, and I feel like there is no space for me. He pretends to like me and want to talk but I don't feel like he is hearing a word I say."

One time when Michael came back to St. Louis, Dad wanted to take us to Ted Drewes ice cream shop, a renowned gathering place in our city. He insisted on driving my brother Ben's car even though it was a stick shift and he had never driven a manual transmission before. He tore through the yellow lights as they turned red. We were all yelling at him to slow down. The gears crunched and rattled as Dad rammed the car into gear. I looked out the window to see people making drug deals on the corner. Dad didn't care about the car or about our safety. We looked at each other in fear. We didn't want to break down here.

Michael was usually even-keeled but he exploded in anger and surprised me. "If your Dad abused you or hurt you in any way, I don't want him in our lives!" he said, his eyes turning red and filling with tears.

"Let's wait and find out what really happened," I said, worried at the strength of his response.

"You need to go to therapy," he said.

"But I'm scared to find out."

"I understand," he said. "I really do, but this is not going away on its own. It's been happening for a while and it's not going to stop until you find out the root cause." I was pacing across the room at this point.

"All right," I said reluctantly. "I'll see if I can find someone."

I was hoping a therapist could somehow help me to feel better without finding out what happened. I wanted the memories, whatever they were, to stay hidden forever.

Marilyn

1961

In November of 1961, her first-grade teacher Ms. Ernestine Strothkamp spoke to me. Ms. Strothkamp was lean, kind, and caring as well as flustered by having all the mischief makers in first grade dumped on her.

"Laurie doesn't belong here," she said. She's very bright. I'm recommending she go in the fast track. She can't learn anything here with all these acting out children."

I didn't realize at the time that going from the lowest to the highest level of first grade was like entering first grade two months late. So, I didn't tutor Laurie or even ask if I should. Since my mother was such an interference with my two older sisters, I didn't want to butt in, but that attitude was soon to change.

About one month after Laurie was placed in the "fast" track, the principal, Ms. Elvira Prudhomme, called me into the office.

"Laurie isn't doing well. We think she'd be more comfortable going back to the "slow" track."

Ms. Prudhomme was six feet, the same height that Laurie would reach at maturity. She was a spinster who ran a taut ship. Her arms hung down like those of a football player. Parents and teachers seldom crossed Ms. Prudhomme.

Furious about this wavering, I said, "Laurie was recently tested in a research study, and she ranks in the top two percent of intelligent individuals in this country. I've made my decision."

Laurie continued in the "fast track" but always had a complex about her ability, until graduate school. It was not until June 1, 2003 that I understood why the teachers in kindergarten thought she was dumb. Suddenly it all made sense why Laurie had changed her behavior so radically. At three, Laurie went from being an angel to a hellion at home, but not at nursery school. At six she nearly died.

Chapter Two

Susie Midada

Dad and me

"The main reason I'm so passionate about peace," Dad told me one time, "is because we are all the same. Near the beginning of my time in the war, I was walking up a hill on the front lines in Germany. When I was almost at the top, a young German soldier came into view. We both drew our guns at the same time. He looked just like me. He was about my age, 19, thin, tall and he had the same hazel eyes and brown hair. He looked terrified and so was I." Dad paused remembering his terror.

"I saw an image of his mother crying when she found out he died. I could feel her pain and it was unbearable. We looked deeply into each other's eyes, and at the same moment, we both lowered our guns and walked away."

Dad joined the army in 1942, a young Jewish man passionate about rescuing the world from Hitler's grasp. They trained him to climb mountains in Italy and go behind enemy lines. He was fluent in Italian and in one small village in Italy he met a young woman. "She wanted to marry me," Dad said. "But I was not ready for that yet. When I pulled away in the back of a truck, she ran after me screaming waving a white handkerchief."

"Bernardo, Bernardo!"

"It broke my heart."

Dad was so moved by that moment in his life that he created a testament to it. When I came to visit and it was time to leave, he would run after my car madly waving a white handkerchief. My siblings and I dubbed it the "white handkerchief treatment".

Toward the end of Dad's life, he was asked to give a speech about his years in the war and talk about the medals he had received, the purple heart and the silver star. Dad wrote a note to his brother after the event expressing his feelings.

What they didn't mention in the citations was the young lieutenant who died in my arms gurgling blood on the little fat boy,

> *Poochie, whose foot was blown off by a mine because I talked him into going on a reconnaissance mission to join up with another company that our company was relieving on the Front Lines. The honors I received were great, but the memories aren't so hot.*

When Dad came back from World War II, he spoke out against the war before it was popular to do so. He also became good friends with a famous peace researcher in St. Louis and worked with him for years. I went to the March on Washington in 1968 protesting the Vietnam War with Dad and his cousin. It was one of many protests we attended together.

From the moment Mom was born, strangers stopped on the street to comment on her beauty. She had curly blonde hair, startling blue grey eyes, and a slender frame. Grandma Maya would always brag about Mom's beauty to her friends. Mom modeled hats and bathing suits as a young adult, but she hated the focus on her looks. She wanted people to look past her beauty to the person inside. She was even offered a modeling contract in New York but turned it down to stay in St. Louis and marry Dad.

Dad, Bernard (Bud) Goodman, was the oldest of three boys and Mom, Marilyn Probe, was the youngest of three girls. They met through the St. Louis Jewish community and their families knew each other from the time they were young. When they started dating in 1952, Dad's younger brother Daniel had just died. He was the pilot in a small plane and made the decision to go up in bad weather and crashed. Dad was devastated and Mom listened as he poured out his pain. She told me many years later his vulnerability during that time is what initially attracted her to him.

Mom wrote in her journal:

> *I had a gut feeling when I walked down the aisle that it was not a good decision to marry him. But I wanted to marry him anyway because I was so in love with him.*

My parents were completely and passionately in love and that love continued (even though it changed forms) throughout their lives.

For Mom's birthday one October, about five years after they had divorced, Dad sent her a dozen roses with a note telling her how much he loved her. He also told me once near the end of his life that Mom was the love of his life. No one else ever came close. Mom visited Dad when he was in the last year of his life in the nursing home and often fed him dinner when he could no longer feed himself. She told me she had forgiven him a long time ago for any of his faults.

Mom modeling a hat circa early 1950s

Being in the kitchen with Mom as a young child was a challenge. She was constantly forgetting she had things on the stove and wandering off. I would pull on her skirt to show her the burning pan and she would snap out of her reverie by tossing it into the sink just before it burst into flames. Crying was the best way to get her attention. She would ask me what was wrong but once I calmed down, she was unreachable again, off in another place far, far away. It felt like she was a mirage, a carbon copy of a person, like she had no substance, and my hand could go right through her body like it was air.

Dad was too present. His presence sucked the energy out of the room until there was no space for me. He was tall and loud and wild. He liked rough housing with me, playing all kinds of games. He was in my bubble, so focused that it was hard for me to breathe. Sometimes it was fun, kind of, and nothing bad would happen. But just when I let down my guard, he would touch me too hard, too strong. My stomach would jump because it felt wrong, my gut twisted, and it hurt. Fun turned into scary faster than a spinning top. I was cautious, wary.

Some days Dad would lay in bed for hours and not get up all day, but other days he was full of energy. He woke me up in the morning with reveille, just like they did in the army, his hands curled in front of his face in the shape of a trumpet, his fingers moving up and down as he sang the tune:

It's time to get up,
It's time to get up,
It's time to get up in the moooorrrrrning.

"Oh Dad," I would say half-heartedly. "Stop that. I'm up." Dad would continue with "I am the Monarch of the Sea" from the H.M.S. Pinafore (1878):

Dad:
I am the monarch of the sea,
The ruler of the Queen's Navee,
Whose praise Great Britain loudly chants.
And we are his sisters and his cousins and his aunts!

Me:
And they are his sisters and his cousins and his aunts!

Together:
His sisters and his cousins whom he reckons by the dozens and his aaaaaaauuuuuunnnts!

One night when I was five, Dad came home from his work in the home goods family business and dumped piles of toys and candy for me as well as clothes for him all over the couch. I pounced on the toys and candy with delight.

"These things cost too much money," Mom said, frustrated he hadn't asked her first.

"I'll buy what I want," Dad said dismissively. "Get off my back."

"But we don't have the money." Mom said. "Why do you do this?" she screamed.

"I don't have to take this," Dad said and stormed out.

"He knows we don't have the money. I'm going to return it." Mom told me. I tried to grab a toy off the couch.

"What are you doing?" She turned her full fury on me screaming, the veins standing out on her neck like green snakes,

"I'm returning that! Get your hands off it!"

I cowered and ran out the door to the backyard. The beautiful forest behind my house was my refuge. Escaping into nature was my spiritual haven. I would lean into the trees and feel their strength seep into my bones. Sitting on the back porch, I watched the thunderstorms roll through. The lightning lit up the sky like a huge exclamation point silhouetted against the darkness, and the thunder boomed out of nowhere like rolling stones reflecting the intensity of my feelings of rage and helplessness.

But my best connection was with the moon. From my second-floor window, I had the perfect perch on my bed to see the moon at night as it rose over my neighbor's house standing guard for me. When I was in pain and had no one to turn to, the moon shone its light upon me, touching my body with tendrils of soft, gauzy strands that entered my heart and filled me with peace. I basked in the moonlight and let it cradle me with its tenderness.

When Dad came back home, he walked into my bedroom where my younger sister Shira was asleep in her crib.

"Do you want me to tell you a story?" he whispered.

"Yes," I said eagerly. Tell me a Susie Midada story." Susie was small, the size of Tom Thumb, and she was always getting into trouble and then miraculously escaping.

"Susie went into the ice cream shop on the shoulder of her friend Coldfoot the Camel," Dad began. "Coldfoot got his name because he always had cold feet in bed and no one wanted to sleep next to him. Coldfoot tripped on his way up to the counter and Susie flew off his shoulder into the milkshake machine. Susie screamed for help, but Coldfoot didn't hear her. Coldfoot put in his order for a vanilla shake which was his favorite."

"That is my favorite too," I said eyes shining. "Poor Susie Midada. How scary!"

"The young man started making Coldfoot his shake. Susie's friend Middie the Mouse was there at the shop. She heard Susie's screams and scampered down into the milkshake machine when the man's back was turned scooping out the ice cream. Susie jumped on Middie's back and Middie climbed up the twisted blades and got Susie out of there. They were on the counter when the worker turned around, saw the mouse, and started screaming. Middie dashed across the counter with Susie holding fast…"

"What happened next?" I asked breathlessly.

"I will finish the story tomorrow. Time for sleep," he said. Dad loved cliffhangers like the Saturday matinee movies he went to as a child. I loved Susie Midada with all my heart. I knew that if she could survive her problems, so could I.

Mom and Dad circa 1963

Marilyn

1963

Bud thought he had married a quiet introvert, a malleable virgin. I was a virgin. I married someone I thought had a backbone as I felt my Dad, whom my Mom controlled, was weak. I didn't want a weak husband. I thought that was what led to so much tension and arguments in our household. Little did I know Bud would try to out argue me. Stubborn as I was, I just sharpened my mind on his. I got release by yelling at our children after Bud slammed the door and walked out. Bud would conclude our brief disagreement to my frustration with the words, "I never argue, I only discuss."

He was very frustrated he could not control me. He said, "There can just be one boss, and I am it."

Chapter Three

Civil Rights

I was raised with parents who believed deeply in the cause of civil rights. When I was in third grade, I went with Dad to a protest at the Jefferson Bank in downtown St. Louis because they weren't hiring any black people. He hoisted me up on his shoulders so I could survey the crowd. There was a feeling of anger and frustration in the air. I felt a part of something important, the seeds of change. My father was good friends with Percy Green who was a member of the Black Panthers and led a group called Action Committee to Improve Opportunities for Negroes (ACTION). Percy found out many of the CEOs and executives of corporations that refused to hire blacks were involved in a St. Louis white elitist secret society called the Veiled Prophet.

Each year they would vote in one of the upper-class white men to be the prophet, and he would wear a veil in a special parade and preside over a debutante ball. Dad helped Percy organize a protest where several members of ACTION snuck into the ball and a young woman from the group flew from the balcony on a cable line onto the stage and tore the veil off the prophet. Unveiled, the prophet could now be recognized. This subversive act brought to the forefront the classist roots of the event from its inception.

Mom also was active in civil rights and a member of the Freedom of Residence committee in St. Louis that was spearheaded by her friend, Ruth Porter. They worked tirelessly for the rights of black people to own whatever home they chose. An interracial couple was denied the right to buy a home and, with the help of Freedom of Residence, the couple sued the real estate company. In 1968, this led to the mandate that all housing had to be made available for purchase by African Americans. This accelerated a phenomenon which was already happening in St. Louis, spurred on by the 1954 Brown vs. Board of Education verdict of forced desegregation, called "white flight," where middle class white people moved from the inner-city neighborhoods to the suburbs.

In 1963, the summer between my third and fourth grade year, we moved to 11 Princeton Place in a suburb of St. Louis called University City. My younger sister Shira was 5 years old and my brother Ben was 2. My parents picked this specific suburb because it was adjacent to the City of St. Louis, still racially and economically diverse, and not far enough out of the city to be affected by white flight. Our neighborhood was called University Heights and all the names of the streets were named after Ivy League universities. Most people who lived there were white. The homes were built for the wealthy and elite back in the early 1900s and they were all oversized mansions, some with carriage stones still in front of them. The old growth oak trees towered above the houses like sentries, protecting us. There was a chain across the end of the street to prevent drive-through traffic. My siblings and I spent a lot of the time outside playing games like Kick the Can and Hide and Go Seek with the neighborhood children.

Our home at 11 Princeton Place

Perched on top of 25 stairs with two green rolling hills and four elegant white pillars, our house was the epitome of a southern mansion. There was a grand entryway with a green and white checkered floor pattern, where I roller skated and Dad and I often danced, opening onto a large winding staircase with plush red carpeting. As an 8-year-old girl, it looked like a castle, and I dreamed of getting married there leisurely walking down the broad staircase to greet my handsome husband.

Shira, Ben and I loved to slide down the banister of the staircase backwards when Mom wasn't looking. She told us it was off limits, but it was just too tempting. As a concession to our need for play, Mom had our handyman hang a rope from the ceiling in the dining room and build two sawhorses with a flat piece of plywood on top with gym mats on the floor. We jumped onto the rope from the sawhorses and after swinging to our hearts content, landing on the mat. That kept the three of us occupied for hours. Mom kept the rope up during parties at our house as a conversation piece.

About three blocks away from our home was a neighborhood called "The Loop." The Loop was an interesting juxtaposition of several up-and-coming restaurants, movie theatres and boutique stores along with crumbling rundown brick tenements. Most people who lived there were black. My parents did not want us raised in a homogeneous environment, so this was their compromise.

When I started Hanley Junior High School, I got the nickname "Goody." I hated that name. My last name was Goodman and I was a bit of a goody two shoes even though I wouldn't admit it. I didn't drink or smoke or party and believed in playing by the rules. I went to classes, worked hard and kept my head down.

I could only wear my clothes for a short time before my pants and shirt sleeves were not long enough anymore. One time in sixth grade another child asked me:

"How tall are you?"

"8 foot 4," I said.

I meant 4 foot 8, but I felt like 8 foot 4. I was soaring towards my final height of six feet. Like any teenager, I wanted to fit in. When I went home and complained to Mom, she told me to be proud of my height, keep my head up high and put my shoulders back. I listened and have always had good posture. In high school, when I came home crying one day because only three boys in the school were taller than me, she told me that if the boys were worried about me being taller than them, they weren't worth dating anyway. That advice came in handy later in life.

Mom and Dad were also on the forefront of the movement that required bussing black children to all white schools to ensure integration. When the bussing laws passed, my parents had one of the first integrated parties in St. Louis to celebrate.

In the late 1960s, however, Hanley Junior High School was a hotbed of racial angst. Lockers were set on fire. Fights broke out in the halls. Every day was like a powder keg waiting to explode.

Integration sounds like a simple idea but placing people from different socio-economic and cultural backgrounds into one school and hoping everyone got along was like a social experiment with no one there to educate us. We clumped into groups hanging out with those who looked like us and were culturally compatible. I didn't understand why so many of my black classmates were angry. I had no clue about white privilege and what it was like to have to deal with prejudice and racism day in and day out.

Ann was a short, dark, black girl with a light brown afro and huge angry eyes. She stood up and announced to everyone in the class one day: "Laurie is scratching her butt."

The whole class laughed. I didn't say anything and neither did the teachers. After that, Ann knew I was fair game and came after me taunting and teasing me whenever she could. I had a hard time resolving within me the excitement and passion of being a part of the civil rights movement and the tension of being in an integrated junior high school. I knew that civil rights was a very important cause and believed that all human beings were equal. At the same time, I was angry because I felt my parents' passion for civil rights trumped their love for me.

I overheard Mom on the phone one day talking to Ann's mother about discrimination at the school because of tracking policies. They both agreed that black students were put into the lower tracks to segregate them. I knew my parents liked Ann's parents and believed they would take Ann's side if I told them about the bullying, so I never did.

One day soon after I started high school, I saw Ann in the hall. She walked up to me and pushed me.

"Stupid, ugly white girl," she said. A surge of newfound confidence rose within me.

"Don't touch me," I said. I moved forward ready to fight and met her eyes with a fierce determination. To my surprise she ran off and never bothered me again.

After our junior high years, we all melded together better at University City High School. There was a solidarity with black and white students alike. In 1972, we staged a sit-in and refused to go to class after a black teacher was fired because he wanted to include black literature in the curriculum. We won the protest, and he was rehired and allowed to include the course.

In 1973, my senior year, I won the coveted part of Charity in the musical *Sweet Charity.* Dad, who taught me musical songs from the time I started talking, helped me with my audition piece and rehearsed lines with me. I was fortunate enough to have three leading men who were all friendly, gracious and naturally talented actors. In one scene, I kissed Anthony. He was significantly shorter than me so we decided it would be best if we kissed sitting down. I was nervous because I had never kissed a man before; I hadn't even been on a date. Anthony and I "practiced" quite a bit and he was a wonderful teacher. His girlfriend had daggers darting out of her eyes from the chorus when we kissed.

I loved playing Charity. She allowed me to be sexy, confident and full of life. After a successful opening night with my whole family in attendance, they all hugged and congratulated me except my mother's mother, Grandma Maya, who hung back. When all the hubbub died down, Maya, walked up to me scowling.

"Why did you kiss that short, dark, black man?" she asked. "You should have kissed the tall, gorgeous mulatto man."

The gorgeous mulatto man was Carter and one of the few men taller than me at the school. I guess even though Carter was black, his height and lighter skin made it okay in Grandma's eyes to kiss him. I swiftly came to Anthony's defense.

"Grandma," I said. "I would love to kiss both of them, but I only get to kiss Anthony. Anthony is one of the nicest people I have ever met. Stop talking about him that way!"

Marilyn

1966

Bud, too, I thought at the time, was such a wonderful father. He played with the children under my tutelage, bathed them each as babies. They played games together. He sang with them. We took trips to state parks and saw Shakespeare at Stratford-on-the-Avon in Canada. Bud was like a pied piper with not only ours, but everyone's children.

He was so good with children that I often felt left out, but I was compensated by the feeling that I was lucky to be married to someone who cared so much about his offspring. Buddy and I gave great parties, were a wonderful dance team, had the same political beliefs and supported each other in our radical causes, against the war in Vietnam, supporting fair housing and public accommodations. Perhaps our strong involvement in politics and civil rights served to mask the storm brewing between us.

Chapter Four

Roots

Circa 1920s: my mother's mother is on the far right in the back row

I come from a long line of Jews who have never married outside the faith. My great-grandfather on my mother's side came to St. Louis from Russia. He became a prominent rabbi in the Jewish community. He had seven children; my grandmother Maya was the oldest girl.

I also come from a strong line of matriarchs. Even though the business was in her husband's name, Maya was the driving force behind its success. Starting at 8 years old, I often visited Grandma Maya at work on Saturdays in downtown St. Louis. Maya worked well into her 80s. She had a small printing shop with a glass door on a busy street. Opening the door in the main room, I was hit with a variety of clanking, hissing and grinding noises as the presses spit out paper as fast as BB gun pellets. The ink smelled pungent like a strong bitter medicine that you wouldn't want to taste. I loved to stand at the end of the press and watch the paper come out. The different colors on the brochures were blurred together as they flew off the press and made a thunk sound as they hit the stopper at the end. Grandma let me sit on a stool and collate the papers into piles.

Afterwards, I would spend the night at her house. She slept in a separate room from my grandfather on the second floor of their home with a colorful quilt on the bed and well-worn wooden floors. We would sit on the bed together propped up against feather pillows and she would show me how she curled her hair when she was young with torn off strips of rags that she wound around thick brown tresses. She talked to me about how important it was to be financially independent as a woman. I knew Grandma was wealthy and I wanted to be rich too, so I hung on to every word. She was intimidating to some but not to me. We always got along well which made it even more painful when we had two major conflicts just before she died.

In the summer of 1983, I was planning my wedding which would be in August. Maya called me very upset.

"Laurie, you need to get married by a rabbi. Even though you are marrying a Jewish man, you won't *really* be married unless you are married by a rabbi."

"Grandma, there are no rabbis in Ashland, Oregon and it isn't important. We found a Unitarian minister to marry us, and I like him."

"Find a rabbi in another town and I will pay for you to go up there and have him perform a ceremony."

"I don't want to go to another town to get married by a rabbi," I insisted.

"It's important to *me*. If you don't get married by a rabbi, you will lose your inheritance," she said menacingly. She had told me she would give me several thousand dollars.

"Fine!" I screamed. "I don't care about your inheritance anyway."

"Send back my pearl bracelet. I don't want you wearing it at the wedding," she said.

I sent the bracelet back.

Later Mom told me that Maya was upset she couldn't attend my wedding because it was too far away from St. Louis, and she was not well enough to fly. That didn't even occur to me at the time.

Now that I'm closer to Maya's age, it would hurt me too if I couldn't attend my grandchild's wedding. I didn't even consider getting married, as many brides do, in their hometown. Long gone were the days of wanting to walk down the stairs of my childhood home into the arms of my husband. When I left St. Louis to move out west, I had no desire to go back. My parents didn't offer to help pay so we paid for the wedding ourselves. My sister told me later that Mom and Dad offered to pay for her wedding and engagement party so she would get married in St. Louis and they could invite their friends. I should have considered at least an engagement party in St. Louis where my family could attend. But I don't remember my grandmother, parents or me bringing up that possibility.

In addition, like many people near death, my guess is that Maya was worried that she had not been loyal to her faith. The first-born girl of a rabbi, since I had known her, she didn't go to synagogue, keep the Sabbath, or celebrate the major Jewish holidays. I'm not sure how my getting married without a rabbi played into her fears. Possibly she had not taught me well enough how to be Jewish or as a grandchild I was an extension of her.

Regardless, if I had it to do over again, since there was no Jewish community or rabbi in Ashland at the time, I would have taken the trip north to the closest large town Eugene, Oregon with my fiancée and had a short ceremony with a rabbi to appease her. It would have made her happy and I could have gotten the money—a win-win. But I was young, headstrong, and stubborn.

I visited her one last time in December of 1983, five months before she died. I was sitting next to her bed chatting with her when in the middle of a sentence she couldn't talk any more. She was terrified and so was I. I found out later that she was having a transient ischemic attack (TIA). It is a warning that you are in imminent danger of a stroke. Her voice came back after what seemed like an eternity but was probably only five minutes.

"Laurie," she said, "Please stay the night with me. I'm scared."

"No Grandma. I can't. I have other plans. Sorry." I didn't know this would be the last time I saw her.

I went home for her funeral and the immediate family members went over to her apartment afterwards. This was the big moment everyone had been waiting for. Mom was there with me, Shira and Ben, her two sisters, and their children and grandchildren.

We all went up the elevators together to her luxury apartment on the top floor. The tension was palpable, almost scary. We burst through the door and into the hall, and people began running. They ran into her bedroom and yanked open her jewelry box stuffing rings, necklaces and earrings with emeralds, diamonds and pearls into their pockets and purses. They went into her walk-in closet grabbing clothes off the hangers. They were looting her apartment.

Grandma's first painting

In the midst of this feeding frenzy, I sat on her bed in shock, tears rolling down my face. I could still feel her energy there. I told her I loved her and asked if she could forgive me for not staying with her that night. Then I calmly walked over and took the one painting of hers I wanted off the wall. Maya started painting in her mid-70s and the painting of an Indian woman from a National Geographic photo was her first painting.

My father's side of the family also had a strong matriarch, my great-grandmother Ruth. Ruth started a home goods business which became the family business for two generations. She had two children and her oldest boy was my grandfather Isaac.

My great-grandfather on my father's side came through Ellis Island from Lithuania with his wife and young daughter Lillian (my grandmother) in 1906. He moved to a small town in Illinois called Hillsboro where he started a general store. It was here that Isaac met Lillian when he was showing samples of his sheets, blankets, and towels to sell in the store. He married her and whisked her off to St. Louis.

Lillian's mother had a nervous breakdown in 1923 when their store went out of business, was diagnosed with dementia praecox, hebephrenic type (later the name was changed to schizophrenia), and died in the mental hospital in 1936. No one ever talked about her, and I didn't find out about her mental illness until I discovered a poem Mom wrote after her death.

When Isaac and Lillian got married, they lived with Isaac's mother Ruth. Ruth had a strong domineering personality and there was no space for Lillian in her house. Lillian finally gave Isaac an ultimatum and they moved into their own home. Lillian played the piano and Isaac, in addition to the family business, played the violin in the orchestra for silent films. I heard they were both talented musicians, but never had the chance to hear their music. After Dad's youngest brother Daniel died in a plane crash in 1953, two years before I was born, they never played their instruments again.

Artist genes were passed down to me which inspired my love for acting, singing, writing and learning and falling in love with American Sign Language. The family business genes from the strong matriarchs, Maya and Ruth, helped me become successful when my husband and I decided to start our own Amway business.

When Mom was not off in her own world, she would fight with Dad. Many altercations resulted in Dad leaving and her screaming at one or more of the children. I felt captive to her anger. It was like living inside a roller coaster. I never knew when it would start up again and emotions spun out of control. I would lie in bed flat on my back at night when I heard my parents screaming at each other. I believed that if I lay there long enough in that one position then they would stop fighting sooner. Calm times were still rife with tension. We held our breath waiting for another outburst that could happen at any moment.

Dad constantly put Mom down saying she was a women's libber and he should be in charge.

Although I didn't see him hit Mom, he liked arguing with her. He liked arguing with anyone about everything taking the role of the devil's advocate. He would go on spending sprees and bring home buckets of toys, candy and ice cream for us. Even though we liked it, there was something sinister about it, like he was wanting something from us in return.

It didn't occur to me when I was growing up that my parents were mentally ill. I just thought I lived in a volatile household.

In December of 2001, I flew back to St. Louis for the 50th wedding anniversary party of some dear friends of mine, Mitch and Carol. I was used to Michael driving to the airport, but this trip I was alone. I missed the turn off, went the wrong way across the Bay Bridge and had to turn around at Treasure Island. When I finally got to the airport parking lot, I ran into the bathroom, had a panic attack and could barely breathe. I pulled myself together and tried to put the sexual abuse accusation from Mabel, the psychic healer, out of my mind. I didn't want to think about the turmoil of emotions going on inside of me.

I met Mitch and Carol when I had a crush on their son, James. One fall day in 1972 during my junior year of high school, James was walking home after school with his brother Larry who was carrying a dead cat in a plastic bag. I caught up with them and started asking about the cat which Larry explained he was dissecting for his biology class. When we arrived at their Tudor home with front-facing gables and tall thin windows, his mother Carol answered the door with an ashtray balanced on her head and a silly grin on her face. She was about five feet tall with black hair and piercing gray eyes. I liked her immediately. Mitch, a short thin man with salt and pepper hair and metal spectacles, came up behind her assessing the situation and saying brightly "Look what the cat dragged in!"

Carol was a psychologist who saw clients in the basement of her home. Mitch worked for Eagle Stamps, stamps you received after shopping at the local department store, Famous and Barr, and could then paste in a small stamp book and exchange for products of your choosing. In his spare time, Mitch drew wonderful cartoons which he submitted to the St. Louis Post Dispatch, but they were never published. I wish I had saved some copies.

Their home was calm and welcoming, full of humor, and a great respite from the turmoil of my abode. Even though James had no interest in a relationship with me, we formed a social group with his brother Larry, and some of their friends meeting often at Carol and Mitch's home. We became lifelong friends and still stay in touch. After I left for college, I visited Carol and Mitch faithfully for thirty years whenever I would go back to St. Louis to see family and friends. They loved me like the daughter they never had.

At their anniversary party, I made a speech about how their relationship was inspirational to me in my marriage. While I was there, I remembered a cherished conversation I had with Mitch many years earlier on the red brick front porch of his home just before I left to move out west.

"I have some important advice for you," Mitch said. "It's a good thing to spread your wings, but don't forget your roots. Roots will always be a part of you. There are many people in St. Louis who love you very much. Remember that Carol and I are always here if you need us."

Mom and Dad had divorced in 1981 and Mom was still single in 2001. After the anniversary party, I visited with her at her rental on the fourth floor of a brick apartment building with large windows that looked out over the treetops. She said she liked not having an elevator so she could get her exercise. We swam laps together in the local Jewish Community Center pool across the street and did some yoga. That night she invited some of her friends over and we ate delicious food and laughed. I felt comfortable and at ease.

Two years after the divorce, Dad married a woman named Elle whom he met through a personal ad in the newspaper. His ad won "ad of the month" and was featured at the top of the page. Dad was an accomplished writer of several unpublished plays and musicals. Elle, 20 years younger than Dad, quiet and unassuming, was from a small town in southern Missouri.

Ironically, they now owned a small brick tenement (Dad called it a bungalow) in the Loop, just several blocks from the large mansion where we grew up. As I walked up the cracked steps into their living room, I watched the cockroaches scatter. I perched myself tentatively on one of the torn easy chairs and Elle left Dad and me alone to talk.

"I want you to have these after I'm gone," he said. I stared aghast at pictures of me at different ages that he had copied, cut out, and pasted into a scrapbook. He had cut off pieces of my fingers and toes. It looked like an album from a horror movie.

"What do you think happens when you die?" I asked, ignoring the pictures.

"When we die, we die and that is the end," he said. "Ashes to ashes and dust to dust."

"I believe the soul leaves our body and then we are reincarnated and come back again."

"That's ridiculous," he said. "What scientific proof do you have?"

Dad enjoyed taking the opposite point of view. It happened so often that it was hard to know whether he really believed his perspective or just got enjoyment out of disagreeing and winning the argument.

"I don't need scientific proof," I said. "This is spiritual, not scientific."

"Do you have to be human?" he asked. "Can you come back as an ant or a dog?"

"Humans come back as humans," I said. "But not right away. During the time between lifetimes, we have the capability to see what is happening in our loved one's lives and help guide them if we choose."

"Nonsense," Dad said. "When we die, we decay and that is it."

I'd always been fascinated with what happens after you die. It is ironic that Dad did not believe in reincarnation but his mother was the first to introduce the concept to me. Grandma Lillian was all softness, warmth and smooth edges, the opposite of Grandma Maya's dynamism and ambition. I was her first grandchild, a girl. After she gave birth to three sons, she was delighted to have a granddaughter. Like Grandma Maya, one of the most vivid memories I have of her is related to my hair. She loved to brush my naturally curly auburn hair which I inherited from her.

One day when I was about 10 years old, I asked her about the painting that hung above her couch.

"That's Nell Gwynn," she said. "Nell started out selling flowers in front of the Elizabethan Theatre in London and then she became a famous actress and eventually was the mistress to King Charles II. I believe I was reincarnated from Nell Gwynn," she told me.

Grandma's painting of Nell Gwynn
—Artist: Gottfried Kneller

"What's reincarnation?" I asked.

"Your soul, the essence of who you are, doesn't die with you," she explained. "When a baby is born your soul goes inside that new person and you come back again for another life. I was Nell Gwynn and then I died and came back again as your grandma." I was fascinated by this new piece of information.

After Grandma Lillian passed away in 1987, I inherited the painting which I have discovered is an original from the 17th century.

Marilyn

1954

So what was our home life like that we precipitated such devastation to such a young child? What was my husband like and who was I?

I married Bernard (everyone called him Bud or Buddy), an eldest sibling, because I was attracted to his body, his fascinating literary mind, and loved the welcoming arms of his mother who had just lost her youngest son. Bud was A.B.D. (all but dissertation) in Romance languages. He had taught French and Italian at the University of Wisconsin before he dropped out. I bragged that he played the guitar. He played one song "Greensleeves." Since his nose job, he was quite handsome. I had known him since he was nine and sat on his mother's lap at Miami Beach. I was pleased his family would give him $10,000 as a down payment on a house for us.

My Mother's Advice by Marilyn Probe
September 8, 2003

Stop, don't marry him,
He has a history of mental illness
Too old. His grandmother from Hillsboro Illinois
When the mines went belly up and the store
Had no hope and fell into the pit
His grandmother went wild and they threw her
Into a mental institution

He is seven years older, too bold
He has his nose made over
You are too pure, too innocent
You are wooed by his French and Italian
His literary words, the New Yorker
He will not replace your first romance
With Charlie Guggenheim

But only replicate the cruel humor
The wish to promote his self
He is driven to prove he is a man
Make money just like my spouse
Who should have played the violin
Or studied the Talmud while I ran the store

Why he is not an institutional man
He is raving mad
Don't be fooled the way he is the
Pied piper with children
He will lead them down the wrong path

His wobbly legs are up to no good
You need someone clean and upstanding
But then he was the perfect son
Flattering my mom, confiding in her
Writing retirement poems for my dad
Seeing that they were respected for
My mom her charm, her card playing

He danced as gently as my dad
We were a team
And I dreaming it would only
Be like dancing in Jamaica
Like a teapot gone happy with whistles

But in the end my mother never
Said I told you so
But she did wonder unbeknownst to me
In the journal I gifted her
Marilyn is so brave to put up with so
Much, she never complains
But I know her heart is filled with needles
Her stance is one of a warrior turned
Into a punching bag.

Chapter Five

The Monster Within

Michael always left town for work at the most inopportune times, and this was no exception. The second week of December 2001 was the coldest it had been since I moved to Sonoma County. Our Meyer lemon plant in the backyard shriveled up, turned brown and the bright yellow lemons froze.

Coming back from errands, Noah, Rachel and I could see our breath as we got out of the car and walked into the house. When we entered the house, it was almost as cold as outside. I fiddled with the thermostat, and the heater wouldn't turn on. I tried to light the fireplace by tearing up pieces of paper with shaking hands and placing kindling on top, but the flames would not catch. We found out a year later that we had a gas lighter for the fireplace all along, but it was painted over at the time.

When the repair man finally arrived the next day, he said we needed a new heater and wanted to charge me a fortune. I talked it over with Michael and turned him down. The next day I was finally able to find someone who gave me a decent estimate, but it took several days for him to install it.

The following month, coming home from grocery shopping with Rachel, I asked her to unload the groceries from the back of our gold Honda Odyssey minivan and go in the front door. I started to drive into the garage.

"Mom, stop!" she cried.

I waved her off in frustration and drove into the garage not realizing she was trying to tell me that she had forgotten to put down the hatchback. The open hatchback slammed into the top of the garage shattering the window and causing thousands of dollars' worth of damage.

"What were you thinking?" Michael asked when we were cleaning it all up.

That was the problem. I wasn't. I was so depressed that I didn't want to get out of bed in the morning. Every movement felt like I was moving through sticky dark mud. I had to force myself to eat and spent many nights unable to sleep. I also had chronic vaginal yeast infections. The more I tried to hide from the truth, the more it pounded on my door. It took all my strength to hold it back, but I was losing the battle.

In February of 2002, my cold turned into a sinus infection and then I got bronchitis. I was off work for a few weeks. When I went back to work, I got an ear infection and stayed home. When I finally got well, I decided to get help.

The following week, sitting in the small therapy room on the plush purple couch, my therapist, Paul, sat across from me, notes in hand.

"I'm ready to find out the truth," I said. "I'm tired of fighting. What do I need to do?"

"Why don't we try EMDR," he asked.

"What is that?"

"EMDR stands for eye movement desensitization and reprocessing. When someone is upset, they cannot process things as they do ordinarily," Paul said looking at me kindly from across the room.

"Traumatic moments from the past become 'frozen in time' and remembering a trauma can be as bad as going through it the first time because the images, sights, sounds, smells and feelings haven't changed. EMDR helps the brain process the information so that after the session you will still remember but it will be less upsetting."

"How does it work?"

He handed me some headphones and two discs that I held in each hand. I heard a beep in my right ear and then in my left and simultaneously the corresponding disc vibrated in my hand. He dimmed the lights, and I closed my eyes, feeling a sense of peace and relaxation come over my body. I was bypassing my fear and descending into a place of truth.

The first thing I saw was a small room filled with black gook that had the texture of thick oily tar. Emerging from the middle of the tar was a small hand holding a dusky red rose drooping like someone holding their head down in shame.

"I think that is my inner child down in that gook. Something is very, very wrong," I said.

"What is she telling you?" he asked.

"She says what happened was bad, really bad," I said. "She said Dad touched her in ways that felt wrong and if I want her to come out of the black gook, I need to listen to what she has to say."

"This is a good start," Paul said. "We will do more next week."

I was in shock, still not wanting to believe it. Could this image be real?

Olivia was a spiritual healer I met through my sister Shira. She lived in St. Louis, and we had our first session remotely on the phone soon after my EMDR with Paul.

She had me close my eyes and focus on what was happening inside of me. "What does it feel like?" she asked.

"Like a monster is inside me and I can't get rid of it no matter what I do," I said. "It's weighing me down and eating me up from the inside out."

"Focus on the monster within," she said. I did and the following vision appeared.

While Mom was breastfeeding me as a young baby, Dad slapped her and I pulled off the nipple, alarmed, my eyes wide with shock.

Then I was a bit older, around 2 or 3 years old, and I was eating at the table. Dad and Mom were yelling at each other. I stopped eating because I was no longer hungry.

In the next scene, I was around 6 years old which meant Shira was about 3 years old and Ben was a baby. We were all sleeping in the same room when Dad came in and whisked me out of my bedroom into his bedroom. I was disoriented, not understanding what was going on. Mom was not there in the huge king-size bed.

Dad put me down and lay on top of me. It hurt my lungs and I yelled at him to get up, but he didn't move. I was struggling to breathe and pounded on him with my small fists. He grabbed my wrists and pinned them to the mattress. Exhausted, I stopped struggling and started sobbing, tears pouring down my face. I could feel something hard pressing into my thigh.

After what felt like an eternity, he lifted his body up and I was able to wiggle out from under him and run back to my bedroom. He didn't follow me. I lay on my bed on my stomach, shaken and hopeless. I was trying to figure out what to do. I couldn't tell Mom. I wasn't sure she would believe me and even if she did, she and Dad were fighting all the time. I didn't want to make it any worse. I thought about telling one of my grandmothers, Lillian or Maya, but I didn't want anyone to take me away from my family, so I decided not to say anything.

After the session, Olivia told me to rest and take plenty of time to integrate what had happened. I was completely depleted and could barely move. I stayed on our futon couch in the office for what seemed like hours. I felt bereft, hopeless. How could I have forgotten? Did these horrendous things really happen to me? I was beginning to believe they did. Why would I make something like this up?

I thought I wanted to learn the truth, but now that the truth was coming through, I was not so sure. I wanted to rewind the movie reel of my memories and push them back inside to wherever they had been sitting for the last 40 years. But it was too late.

According to Greek myth, the God Zeus gave a box to Pandora, the first woman on earth, and told her never to open it. But as soon as he left, curious, she opened the lid, and out swarmed all the troubles of the world, never to be recaptured. I had opened my own Pandora's box and could feel the agony of my inner child, Little Laurie, piercing my heart and chilling my soul. It was more pain than I wanted to deal with, more pain than I thought possible to hold. It filled my cells with a freezing, sticky dampness that pulled me down into a dark abyss.

Later that night, after the children were in bed, I told Michael what happened.

"I'm so sorry," he said looking at me with such empathy and caring.

"How can I support you?"

"Just being able to tell you and share what is happening is helpful," I said. "Right now, there is nothing else you can do."

A few nights later, Michael wanted to make love. When he reached over to touch me, I recoiled. My sex drive was gone. I started crying. "It's all right," he reassured me with a strong kind voice. "We're in this together."

"I understand why this is happening, but it doesn't make it any easier," I sobbed.

"You need time to deal with all of this," he whispered in my ear, holding me tight.

I cried in his arms. The truth was revealed, but the journey had just begun.

Marilyn

1954

As a sensual virgin, I also could not wait to get married so I could have sex. I was brought up to believe that God would strike me dead if I had sexual intercourse before I was married. Another reason I became engaged is that I felt so close to Bud when he expressed his devastation and compassionate feeling towards his brother Daniel who was killed in an airplane accident just before I said "Yes, I will marry you." His brother had piloted the plane in an oncoming storm against the controller's advice. "I'll just look around," he said.

Daniel was as brilliant as he was reckless, good-looking and politically radical. I did not know that once married, Bud would rarely reveal his feelings to me again. I did not know that he would repress who he was. In many ways, I did the same. That was the way it was.

CHAPTER SIX

Spiritual Awakening

I don't recall Mom and Dad going to the synagogue when I was growing up. I was raised culturally Jewish which meant we celebrated the Jewish holidays like Passover, Chanukah, Purim and Sukkot. The biggest Jewish holiday of the year is not Chanukah. Many Jewish families succumbed to pressure and get Christmas trees. We were not one of them. The biggest holidays are in September and October. They fall on different dates each year according to the Jewish calendar. Rosh Hashanah comes first and is the Jewish New Year. Yom Kippur comes ten days later and is the Day of Atonement when you fast all day to atone for your sins. We didn't honor these holidays when I was growing up. I didn't ever ask why. I wasn't that interested in celebrating a new year that wasn't January 1st and certainly didn't want to leave school and not eat all day, so I didn't question it.

There are three levels of Judaism, the most devout being Orthodox followed by Conservative and then Reform. We were Reform. Orthodox Jews have strict observance of the Sabbath from sundown on Friday to sundown on Saturday where they can't do any work including cooking. All cooking is done beforehand. Our only nod to the Sabbath was that Mom liked to light the candles on Friday night and sing the Hebrew prayers before dinner. Dad hated her doing it and constantly made fun of her, but she persevered. Instead of sending us to Saturday school at the synagogue, we got together with the Weiss family once or twice a month on Saturdays where Dad and Mr. Weiss told us stories about Joseph and the coat of many colors, Moses and the burning bush, and the sacrifice of Abraham. I had fun on the holidays, thought the stories were interesting and liked the beauty of the candles but did not feel any connection to God or to a higher power greater than me.

Dad encouraged all of us to explore different religions. He told us it was an important part of our education. When I was 7 years old and the babysitter, Mary, offered to take me to church with her, I agreed. I was impressed with the beautiful stained-glass windows and ornate architecture. I opened the prayer book with everyone else and sang the songs, standing and kneeling at the appropriate times. When people started to walk up the aisle, I dutifully fell in line. Mary wasn't watching and by the time she looked up, I was kneeling at the front of the church, opening my mouth for the priest to put a round wafer on my tongue. I walked back to my seat holding the wafer gently in my mouth concentrating with my hands in prayer as I observed others doing.

Mary was horrified when I got back to my seat.

"Spit it out!" she whispered desperately in my ear, her eyes wide with alarm.

I spit it out in her hand. I knew I had done something terribly wrong. But how bad could it be? All those other people were calmly walking up to the front. I had just done the same thing. My stomach churned like a garbage disposal with a spoon stuck in it.

"That sacrament is only for those who have gone to communion and are baptized!" she growled in my ear.

What a strange religion, I thought. Only special people could go up to see the priest. My face turned red and I felt like I was in a steam room where it had become too hot and I had to get out.

"I want to leave," I said and started crying. Mary quickly escorted me out of there. Thus ended the exploration of other religions for the rest of my childhood.

When I left for college in the fall of 1973, a new idea of a higher power was introduced into my life. I didn't have much of a choice about where I went to college. Dad said that University of Missouri was five hundred dollars a semester and that was all he could afford so that was where I was going. The University of Missouri, nicknamed Mizzou, is in the small-town of Columbia about halfway between St. Louis and Kansas City where rolling hills with oak trees show in the autumn their colors of crimson, burnt orange and sunny yellow like a young girl in her first prom dress.

My dorm was a small brick building three stories high nestled among the trees. It was for women only. No males were allowed without signing in and there were strict rules about them having to leave after curfew in the evening. After smoking pot, drinking wine and having a great time, we often hid the men in our closets to evade the resident assistant when we heard her footsteps down the hall. It was a small dorm with only ten rooms on a floor and we shared showers and bathrooms. We got to know each other well.

One woman who stood out to me was Eliza. Eliza was small and thin with a charming smile and long wavy strawberry blonde hair she pulled back with a scarf. She was very philosophical and pulled me into fascinating conversations. One evening we decided to go to a street party. About halfway through the evening, I had been dancing and came back to find Eliza sitting on the curb with her eyes closed and the hint of a smile on her face like she was sharing a joke with someone who was not there. Fascinated, I sat there watching her for a while until she opened her eyes.

"Did you go somewhere special?" I asked teasingly.

"I was communicating with my friend Aurora," she said.

"What do you mean communicating?" I asked.

"Astral projection," she said with a matter-of-fact tone. "You can communicate with anyone, anywhere, anytime just by closing your eyes and visualizing them. I got a message that Aurora needed me and so I took a moment to be with her and send her love." she said.

"How did you get the message?" I asked.

"It was a gut feeling," she said. It felt like Aurora was pulling on my mid-section telling me she needed to communicate with me. Aurora has a certain energy about her, so I knew it was her.

"What did she tell you?" I asked.

"She wanted to let me know that she was okay. She recently left her family, and I hadn't heard from her since."

I wanted to know more but decided not to pry. I was very curious about astral projection and later asked Eliza how she learned to do it. She said she had several books she could loan me. One of those books was called *Living in the Light: A Guide to Personal and Planetary Transformation* by Shakti Gawain.

Born Carol Louisa Gawain, Shakti took on her new name when she visited India and spent some time there. Written in the 1970s, Shakti explained light represents our own inner wisdom, and intuition, and higher self that can be accessed for spiritual guidance. To get in touch with this guidance, she suggested starting with making a small decision before moving on to bigger decisions.

For example, you are deciding where to eat out. Take a few deep breaths and calm your mind. Then visualize the restaurant. If you don't know what it looks like, say the name to yourself. Everything has energy. If the restaurant is right for you, it will feel like a warm, energizing glow. If the restaurant is not right, you will have a sickening feeling in your gut. When you feel successful with the small things, you can move on to bigger decisions like what career move to make or whom to marry.

I started using this technique with every decision I made and really loved it. Eliza and I had long talks into the night about spirituality and what higher power and God really meant to us.

I loved the connections with my intuition and what I sensed was a higher power within me. I wasn't used to anything firm or solid in my life. Whenever I leaned too hard on my family, it felt like things could easily break, fall apart or vanish into thin air. Contacting this inner light, this energy was different. It was always there whenever I needed it like the best friend I could ever imagine combined with a feeling of peace that was like a warm fire inside my heart.

Was this the God I heard people talk about? There was no worry about sin or going to hell, no concern about being judged and no priest or rabbi I had to ask to contact God for me. I didn't have to pray or say "Hail Marys" or sing Hallelujah or take communion or be baptized or study the Torah or learn Hebrew or get my Bat Mitzvah. This higher power was just there all the time anytime I needed it, and I could count on it like the sun rising every morning and the moon coming out every night. Knowing that, I became calmer and content.

In December of 1977, I used the "living in the light" technique to decide where I wanted to do my student teaching. I had a degree in psychology and wanted to use my skills to help others. After much research, I decided to work at the juvenile hall in Boonville, Missouri, about a 30- minute drive west of Columbia. When I visited there, I was drawn to the energy of these teenage boys. Their vulnerability and sensitivity piqued my interest, and I wanted to make a difference in their lives. I knew on an intuitive level that this was the right place for me to work.

Those four months were very special to me, and I quickly formed strong bonds with the boys and talked to Dad about them. Dad asked me if he could come to teach one day. I agreed and was surprised at how well he related to them. He treated them with respect and assumed they were intelligent. He read them Shakespeare and they had deep intellectual conversations. When he left, they hung out of the windows calling his name begging him to come back. It reminded me of the story he told about the woman in Italy during the war running behind the car yelling "Bernardo!"

These young men were yelling "Bernard, please come back!" Dad was a great teacher. At the time I thought that teaching should have been his profession, not the family dry goods business. I saw that day how much talent had gone to waste. Now I am grateful he didn't teach so that he didn't wreak havoc on any other young person's life.

While doing my student teaching, I shared a small red brick home in Columbia with my roommate, Nancy. We had a charming front porch just big enough for two rocking chairs, a small living room, two small bedrooms and a sprawling backyard. Nancy was gorgeous with tousled blonde hair and thin, tan limbs, easy-going and we got along well. We even shared the same boyfriend (but not at the same time). When I first met Frank through Nancy, I was drawn in by his rugged good looks, candid sense of humor and it didn't hurt that he was awesome in bed. We were not in love, but we had lots of fun.

The mid-70s were before AIDS and amid the sexual revolution. I was young and careless and extremely lucky I didn't catch a disease or get pregnant.

I met Cathy through Frank and we liked each other immediately. She was intelligent and interesting, and we spent hours in her bedroom discussing every possible subject: relationships, politics, religion, and family. Her bedroom was all red, red walls with a red velvet cover on her bed. Her 1-year-old daughter Jessica hung out in there with us crawling around the bed and babbling.

"Laurie, you know my husband is in jail. I need more money," she said one day. "Can I borrow some from you? A hundred bucks or so would be great."

"No," I said.

"Any little bit would help," her big, brown eyes pleaded with me.

"I really don't have any extra," I said firmly.

I knew she was using heroin and needed more money to support her habit. I watched her take it sometimes, putting the needle in and seeing the ecstasy on her face. Afterwards she was blissed out and full of intellectual insights. I thought about taking heroin myself. What would it be like? I was smoking pot often and loved that. Was it similar?

When I contacted my higher power within, there was no light around having Cathy in my life. But I didn't care. I went against what I knew was right for me. I didn't want to lose our friendship. I was young, innocent and had no idea how heroin could transform my life and lead me down a path to poverty, homelessness, jail and possible early death. When I spent time with Cathy, an unseen energy wrapped its tendrils around me like an octopus and drew me closer and closer to the heroin needle.

One day in early December, it was bitter cold, and sheets of ice blanketed the streets like thin lace veils. Cathy called me from a funeral of a friend who had just overdosed on drugs.

"I called my house to check on Jessica and no one is answering the phone," she said.

"Would you please go over there? I'm worried."

When I walked up the many steps to her apartment on the back side of a large Victorian home, no one answered the door. It was unlocked, so I let myself in. There was a man passed out on the floor. Jessica sat in the middle of a pile of Legos and Barbie dolls, her face scrunched up bright red and stained with tears. I reached down to pick her up and noticed her diapers were soaked through and were no longer able to contain the onslaught of liquid. I scurried around opening cupboards and couldn't find any more diapers.

After checking briefly to make sure the man on the floor still had a pulse, I made the decision to take Jessica to the store with me which was only a couple of blocks away. Bundling her up for the cold, we went back down the wooden slatted steps and started to walk down the steep, icy driveway. My fancy looking lace-up tan boots were as smooth as a marble floor on the bottom. I tried to find the dry spots and was doing well until the very end. I lost my balance on a slick patch and slid down towards the street.

What happened next felt like a slow-motion movie. I made it all the way down to the sidewalk and was about to take a huge gasp of relief when I slipped into the street. This moment was a culmination of bad decisions and associations. The house was on a blind curve and as the cab came around the corner and hit me, I lost consciousness.

When I woke up, I was in the hospital bed with my leg levered above me held up by two ropes on either side. Mom stood looking down at me with love and concern.

"Hi Mom," I said groggily.

"It's broken," I said looking at my leg sadly. Memories of the accident came flooding back into my mind. "Where is Jessica?" I asked in a panic.

"She's fine," Mom said. "She landed on the hood of the cab and wasn't hurt at all."

"Oh my God! I can't believe I let her go." I buried my head in my hands. "Can I see her?"

"No," Mom walked towards me and put a warm hand on my shoulder. "Cathy doesn't want to bring her here." I felt responsible and at least wanted to talk it through with Cathy and see for myself that Jessica was all right. At the same time, I was incredibly grateful that Jessica was unharmed. I don't think I would ever have been able to forgive myself if anything had happened to her.

My left femur was broken and the doctor told me I may not be able to walk again and certainly would not be able to run. Instead of a plaster cast, they put a metal pin down the middle of my femur and gave me a smaller cast with Velcro that I could take on and off. The intense pain dominated my consciousness, and I worried I was hooked on Demerol. I was in the hospital for a month.

One day Mom came into the hospital room with some get well cards and handed them to me.

"I don't want any more cards," I said. I just want to be able to walk again." I started tearing them up.

"Stop!" Mom cried, grabbing the cards away from me.

I was furious and jealous of everyone who could walk. I was frustrated. I was bored. The one thing I had was time. Friends came to visit telling me intimate details about their lives. But mostly I was alone and had time to think. I thought about my choice to stay and spend time with Cathy when I knew it was wrong. I thought about my schooling and my life and where I was headed. Cathy never visited me in the hospital or called. I decided to let go of the relationship with Cathy. I never saw Cathy or Jessica again.

One day after physical therapy, I eased myself back into bed to get in touch with the light within. This time I heard a voice that said, "We are here to give you guidance so you don't get on the wrong track again."

The voice was deep and sounded like a low chime or bell. It was very clear. I noticed it was one voice, but it used the pronoun we. I took a moment to regroup and respond in my mind.

"Who are you?" I asked.

"We are spirit guides," they said. "We have taken on the task of guiding you through this lifetime."

"How do I know I am not making this up?"

"Well, I guess you could be," the guides responded. "You are feeling the higher powers of light and goodness. It is a wonderful thing, made up or not."

"That's true," I said.

"Why don't you take some time to communicate with us and see what happens? What do you have to lose?"

That rang true for me.

I lay there with my leg up in the air with tears pouring down. I was so overwhelmed and grateful. This was more than just light and energy.

Now I could ask questions and communicate and receive guidance. I decided to trust them and believe they were real. I'm glad I did. They have never led me astray.

I went home to St. Louis to recuperate. My parents had a good friend, a Catholic priest, who would later leave the church because he fell in love. He was a talented painter and painted a portrait of me at 5 years old.

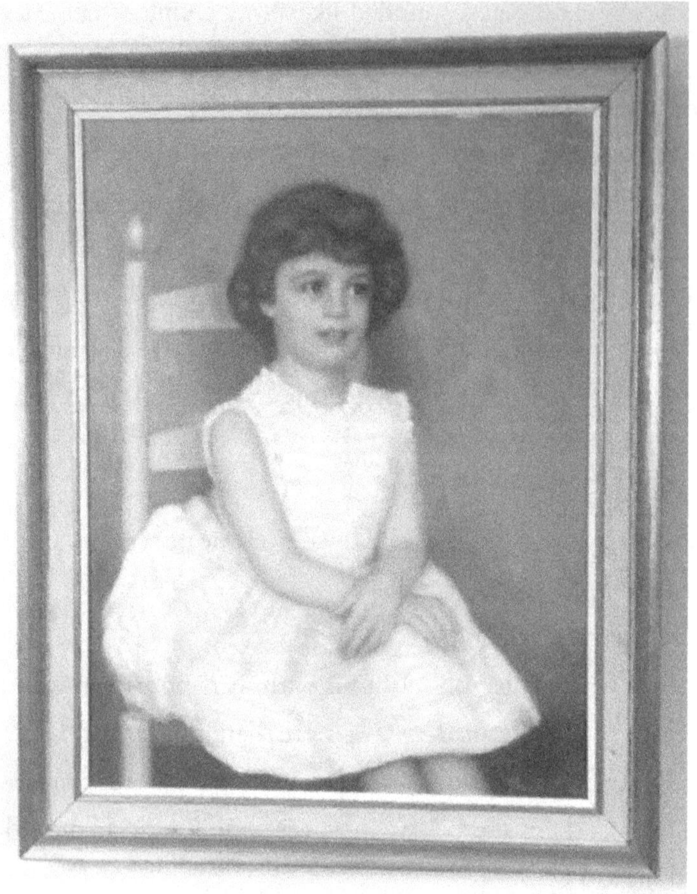

Painting of me at 5 years old

When I got my cast off, he offered to do a healing on me. He put his hands on my leg, and I could feel the heat. "Now try to run," he said. I ran across the lawn, tears pouring down my face.

The biggest gift of this experience was the spiritual awakening it afforded me. I now had a strong connection with my guides and a touchstone within that I could count on. I was able to finish the few things required of me to get my teaching certification and graduate. I decided it was time to leave home and strike out on my own.

"Go west," my guides told me. I had saved some money from my jobs as a school bus driver and radio host. My parents lent me a van and a credit card for gas. Armed with several job interviews, I took off on my next adventure.

Marilyn

1954

After our elaborate wedding ceremony at Washington University Chapel, Bud and I moved to 1077 Jackson in University City, a red brick bungalow with false outside shutters, painted green. University City was Bud's birthplace. We were a stone's throw from Hanley Junior High where he had been the singing star of Gilbert and Sullivan's Mikado.

Bud joined his father's firm, eager to be accepted as a "real" man and a successful businessman by his Dad. He traveled during the week selling tablecloths and curtains on the road and on Saturday mornings, he had office meetings at their family store on Washington Avenue in St. Louis.

At first, I was at a loss as to what to do. I had been raised to marry a man who could give me security so I wouldn't have to work every day like my mother and live happily ever after. I came back from our honeymoon in Biloxi, Mississippi and called my Mom.

"Now what do I do?" I asked.

For a while I worked part time where I had before, at the St. Louis Council on World Affairs as a World Politics Discussion Coordinator. Then I became active in the League of Women Voters. Soon our daughter, who was to change our lives and ours hers, was born.

Chapter Seven

Going West

Leaving St. Louis in June of 1978, I headed out on historic Route 66, originally built as a way for truckers to get from Chicago to the Pacific Coast in 1925. It meandered diagonally southwest, going through small country towns. I borrowed my parents' van where I could sleep at night. They generously offered to pay for gas and I was off to find a teaching job out west.

As I drove through an area in southern Missouri called the Ozarks, I opened the car windows so I could smell the sweet fields of wildflowers with bright colors of orange, purple and blue. Near Lebanon, Missouri, I stepped out of the car after I crossed the Gasconade River. The water rushing over the rocks was like a balm to my soul.

I joined the American Youth Hostel in junior high school and went on canoe trips with them in the Ozarks during the summers for many years. During that time, I fell in love with the rivers: the steep bluffs, the hairpin turns, the lazy riffles, the rushing rapids and the elegant birds that flew above us as we paddled. Not knowing what would be around the next bend piqued my curiosity and kept me in a constant state of anticipation. In the time before cell phones, the Ozarks were a magnificent place to escape.

Now it was my time to leave the great state of Missouri and venture out into the world. After not being able to walk for so long, I felt like a lion freed from its cage ready to run free. I loved being alone and at the same time felt the connection with so many who had traversed this road on their life's journey. I trusted my guides to lead me to the perfect location and job.

I left Route 66 and ventured south on U.S. 377, and after driving for almost nine hours, I stopped in Turner Falls, Oklahoma. After closing the back doors to my metal gray van and checking the locks to make sure they were secure, I fell on the mattress into a deep sleep.

In the morning, I opened the doors to a stream that wound through surrounding oak trees, traversed through small rocks and gained momentum before dropping into a glistening pond like the final note to a well-crafted symphony. I slipped on my swimming suit and walked down the stream stopping to sit on rocks and feel the water rushing over me like silk caressing my skin. I reluctantly left Turner Falls vowing to return one day.

Continuing south to Austin, Texas, I swam in the huge outdoor pool in Zilker Metropolitan Park and spent all day luxuriating in the sun. In the same park, they had an outdoor rock concert at Hillside Theater with a light show. Because it was a college town, I noticed many young people and felt at home. I didn't have a job interview there, but Austin was winning the contest as the best town so far on my trip.

I had my first two teaching job interviews in Shiprock, New Mexico and Tucson, Arizona. Both places were barren with no trees in sight. I felt no desire to live there and crossed them off my list.

Spending the night in Bakersfield, I made the long ascent up the state of California on I-5. I was surprised so many people were enamored with California. I found it hot, dry and boring.

My next interview was for a teacher in a small private school called the Rogue Valley Ranch in southern Oregon. Past Redding, California, my drive through the mountains was shocking in its beauty. Growing up in the Midwest, I was transfixed as I went up I-80 that disappeared into the clouds. Arriving at the top of Siskiyou Pass and seeing the view of the Rogue Valley for the first time felt like being in heaven.

As I descended into the town of Ashland, Oregon, my first stop was Lithia Park. As I sat on the lush green grass next to the duck pond, I was watching people play hacky sack when I had an out-of-body experience hovering over the idyllic scene. I hadn't spoken to anyone, interviewed for a job or done any kind of listing of pros and cons. I just knew this was the place.

Esther, the owner of Rogue Valley Ranch, lived in the Applegate Valley just outside of town. When I drove into the valley, I was surrounded by pine trees and the delicious scent of fresh mountain air wafted through the windows. I spontaneously started singing and crying. The feeling of coming home was overwhelming. I had wondered if I would know when things felt right or if it would be a challenge to follow my inner guidance. Now I knew it would be no problem.

I was in awe of Esther's gorgeous home with a courtyard full of purple, red and white flowers and a huge fountain where birds loved to perch. My room had a twin bed with a blue ruffled bedspread, and I made myself at home. Esther fed me delicious food, and I had a new dream of living in the Applegate Valley. Despite her kindness, Esther had an edge to her personality that was off-putting. Our personalities didn't mesh well, and I was glad I was only staying two nights. Esther was intimidating in the job interview, and I didn't hold much hope for getting the job. Regardless, I did my personal best and was proud of my effort.

I didn't have any other interviews scheduled and I was exhausted. I decided to take the northern route back home and regroup. It was a long slog through Nevada to Salt Lake City. I spent a couple of days enjoying the beauty of Wyoming before descending into Nebraska. I knew the moment that the humid air of the Midwest hit my skin that I was getting close to home. I took I-70 across Missouri, back to St. Louis and slept and relaxed for several weeks.

I was shocked to receive the call from Esther that the teaching job at Rogue Valley Ranch was mine. She told me that she had gotten a message that she needed to hire me. She didn't say how or whom she had gotten the message from, and I didn't ask. Maybe my guides were doing extra work on my behalf. In any case, now that it was time to move, I was nervous about going all the way across the country for a job. St. Louis was the only home I had ever known. But I wasn't willing to turn it down.

Grandma Maya gave me several thousand dollars for moving expenses, and before I knew it, I had landed in Ashland. I found a room for rent in a two-bedroom house with a woman named Glenda. The first night I heard her crying in her room. When I asked her what was wrong, she told me she was getting a roommate for the money and didn't want to live with anyone. It was not quite the welcome I had envisioned.

A few weeks before school started, I got the news they were shutting down the school because they didn't have enough students. I was devastated but determined to figure out a way to stay in Ashland. I got work waiting tables at the Kosmon Tree restaurant and put my name on the substitute teacher list. The yellow house phone rang at 6:00 am and I would stumble into the living room to answer it. Glenda was not too happy about this.

Substitute teaching in the schools was painful. My discipline skills were terrible, and the students took full advantage by acting out and making my days totally chaotic. At night, working at the restaurant, people were often drunk and yelled at me, but the weekends were mine. I made friends immediately, volunteered at the local food co-op, hiked in the fresh mountain air, and went to the bars and danced at night. I learned how to read Tarot cards, got past life regressions, and played with Ouija boards. I was having the time of my life.

In October of 1978, I started dating a man named Henry who was eight years older than me, tall, with sandy brown hair. We had known each other for only a few weeks when he asked me to move to Eugene with him.

"Laurie," he said. "You are settling for a substitute teaching job when you could get a full-time job and get paid better. If you come with me, I will help change you for the better." I was confused about what to do, but luckily, I remembered that I had my guides. When I asked them, I got the answer immediately and told him I was staying. We decided we would still date long distance.

Three days later, I found a 3x5 index card on a bulletin board at the local food co-op. It had frayed edges, and the words were written in block letters:

SIGN LANGUAGE INTERPRETER NEEDED:
JUNIOR HIGH SCHOOL IN CENTRAL POINT, OREGON.

My grandfather, Samuel, was profoundly deaf, and Mom lost her hearing later in life as well. I had always been interested in hearing loss and deafness. While I was at the University of Missouri, I took one class in American Sign Language (ASL) at the Missouri School for the Deaf. I decided to interview for the job.

Invisible Loss

BY MARILYN PROBE

April 2006

The world, which I held so lightly in hand,
whirling at will at the end of twine, falters
with my balance, that spins the globe instead,
as hairs stiffen in the ears.

I yo yo back and forth—how to express the feel
of tipping, the lopsided way I perceive—space between
intelligible words that edge more distant each year.

I gape at how syllables shape the lips to discriminate
an E from a B-the effortless way the brain integrates,
so I know we're not going to Rinaldis to drink some ear.

I marvel at those who need no visual clues to hear,
but only to glimpse the spirit. And know
I need to grow, opening wide my heart space
for others who tilt slightly in another way.

Chapter Eight

Interpreting for the Deaf

If it hadn't been for breaking my leg, I wouldn't have met my guides. If I hadn't met my guides, I wouldn't have been inspired to go out west. If I hadn't gone out west, I wouldn't have met Esther and had the interview to work at Rogue Valley Ranch. If Esther hadn't had a feeling she should hire me (and who knows why she did), I wouldn't have moved to Ashland. If I hadn't moved to Ashland, I wouldn't have seen the 3x5 card on the food co-op bulletin board advertising a job for a sign language interpreter. All those coincidences and serendipities along the way created the life I have today.

How much of life is fate and how much is choice? What influenced Esther when we didn't get along to hire me anyway? What if I hadn't been shopping in the food co-op that day in Ashland and glanced over at the bulletin board to find the card? These are questions with no answers. What I do know is going to a job interview at Scenic Junior High School in Central Point, Oregon that day in the fall of 1978 totally changed the trajectory of my life.

Central Point, which I later affectionately nicknamed "Central Pimple" had a population who predominantly worked at sawmills. The smattering of ticky-tacky look-alike tract homes wasn't central to anywhere that I could see. After the beauty and culture of Ashland, with its Victorian homes, Shakespeare Festival, tourist shops, excellent restaurants, gorgeous parks and vibrant nightlife, it was not a place I would choose to hang out. It was in this ordinary town, at this ordinary school where extraordinary things happened in my life.

A thirty-minute drive from Ashland, Scenic was built like a prison with a circle of cement bunkers facing a barren courtyard. The classroom where I had my interview was small with several uncomfortable blue plastic chairs set up in front of a long rectangular table.

Jack, the teacher, was short and stocky, in his early 40s, balding already with sandy brown hair and thick glasses. Heather, the interpreter, was younger, in her mid-30s, average height with long brown hair dressed in a forest green zip-up smock that was her uniform. A dark solid color made an easy background to look at when hands were flying. Their kindness and warmth belied the stark, cold atmosphere of the school. Jack asked me why I was interested in working with deaf children and I told him about Samuel, my grandfather.

I first became interested in working with deaf people when Grandpa Samuel was aloof during family gatherings. He would hide in his room alone while everyone was visiting. I realized that he couldn't hear what people were saying and that is why he made himself scarce. Sometimes I would sneak into his bedroom to join him. Since there was no captioning at the time, he listened to his TV with a cord attached that went into his ear. He would turn the TV off when I came into the room, and we would talk. I think the quiet and having no background noise helped. I would be sure to face him and speak clearly. He would tell me about his life as a little boy, growing up in Germany and the Orthodox Jewish religion. He would ask me all about my life and I would pour out stories of boys and friends and teachers, everything that was in my heart to share.

I didn't know this at the time, but Mom would also lose her hearing later in life and was profoundly deaf in her 70s. She fought for deaf and hard of hearing people's rights and was dedicated to the charities Walk4hearing and the Hearing Loss Association. Her most passionate advocacy was at the synagogue she joined later in life. She told her rabbi many older people couldn't hear well during the services but were too shy to say anything. She begged her to invest in a surround sound system that hooked into people's hearing aids.

After her stroke, when Mom couldn't talk or walk in 2012, the rabbi came to her bedside and told her they finally invested in a sound system due to her years of insistence, and they had a plaque put near the system with her name on it. I was impressed with her passion and advocacy. I wanted to make a difference for people who couldn't hear. I also knew with hearing loss in my family that someday that person could be me.

"Do you know American Sign Language?" Jack asked.

"I took one class a couple of years ago," I said.

"Would you be open to learning on the job?"

"Sure," I said, having no idea what that would mean.

"We just haven't been able to find someone who knows sign language and we need help. I think you would be great working with deaf children. I could use you in my classroom as an aide as well."

"What is the pay?" I asked.

"We could start you at $3.23 an hour," he replied. That was more than what I was making at the restaurant or substitute teaching.

"Can you start next week?" he asked. "We have more deaf students than we expected and we really need the help."

"Yes," I said. And so began a career that would span 41 years.

Many parents of deaf children in southern Oregon did not want to send their children to the only School for the Deaf in the state of Oregon that was a four-hour drive north. It meant their deaf children would live in dorms there and the parents would only be able to see them during school breaks. They also didn't want their child to feel isolated as the only deaf child in a hearing school. Southern Oregon offered an alternative called the magnet program where a dozen deaf students were bussed to one location, Scenic Junior High. Jack would teach them English and history in his small classroom using ASL. Then, they joined the other hearing students in classes like physical education, art, auto mechanics and math with a sign language interpreter.

When I opened the metal door to Jack's classroom on my first day, I was disappointed there were no windows except for one thin rectangular one on the left side of the door. I soon forgot about the uninviting room when a blonde girl came bouncing in, her face flushed from the cold as she signed to a dark-haired young boy. Their vibrant energy was electric and invited me to engage with them. I watched in awe as their whole bodies moved in tandem with their arms to communicate with each other. Their faces were astonishingly expressive like mimes. Time slowed down and I was living in the moment.

They gathered around Jack who was herding them to their seats. I could feel their love for him, the teacher who they could chat with easily and express their thoughts and feelings. He in turn delighted in each one of them, checking in at the beginning of the day with true interest in their lives. It was their haven in a world where many of them were isolated with families who had no interest in learning sign language.

It wasn't fair to me, or to the children, to hire me with so little knowledge of ASL. But this was before sign language interpreting training in colleges, and most interpreters were hearing children who had deaf parents, like Heather. They were called Children of Deaf Adults (Codas). Trained ASL interpreters were an anomaly and not easily found, especially in rural southern Oregon. With no ASL classes in the area, I picked up what I could from Jack, Heather and the kids and studied at night from a book.

The book that Jack and Heather recommended was called, *The Joy of Signing* by Lottie Riekehof, and was a classic at the time. I committed to learning ten signs a night. Unfortunately, there were flaws with my plan. ASL is a three-dimensional language and learning it from a book, which is two-dimensional, meant I often got some part of the sign wrong: the hand shape, location or movement. The use of space around the body, facial expressions and mouth movements are all a part of ASL grammar. One example is identifying the beginning of a concept by raising your eyebrows and ending it by putting your hands down and nodding your head. None of this ASL grammar was in the book, so I didn't learn it.

When I went with the deaf students to the hearing classrooms, I did my best to sign what the teacher was saying and voice what the students were signing. But I was floundering, embarrassed and totally out of my element. I didn't realize learning a language was so hard and I cried almost every night. The kids complained they couldn't understand me. I was frustrated too and ready to give up. Then something unexpected happened.

I fell in love with the deaf students and ASL which had a magic that infused the space it inhabited. I was still incompetent but it was clear this was a language I wanted to learn. The students started to accept me, and we settled into a routine together. Two of the boys, Oliver and Lucas, took wrestling and I interpreted for them by the mats and cheered like crazy when they won. When my hands flowed correctly, I could feel the energy stream between me and them and see the understanding dawn in their eyes. There was no better feeling in the world.

Facilitating communication became my passion. I knew what it was like in my childhood to not have a voice, to not have any power. Now I had the power to give the students' thoughts and feelings a voice and make sure they were heard. It fulfilled a need in me that I didn't even know was there.

I've since gone back to school, studied sign language interpreting and became nationally certified. I follow the deaf students I've worked with over the years on social media and sometimes get together with them in person. I'm incredibly proud of their accomplishments. Each one of them is like a pearl on a necklace over my heart.

Signage for Fear

BY MARILYN PROBE

February 2004

Sun speckled hands define age
the way sun tells shadow and time,
displaying sign, as my hearing fades,

reveling in the cool-breadth of earth
at dawn as sun and moon join hands,
rousing a box turtle to swagger

on sluggish forelegs, yellow bands
highlighted by her gauche moves
like my daughter, an interpreter

at thirty-three, who turned awkward forefingers
into signage for Holly Near, a contrast
to her ignorance when she was three,

when she didn't know to unlock
her hands by her heart, the language
for fear after the night visitor came near.

Perhaps when all my sound is gone, I'll,
flick my fingers open in front of my heart,
my last words unspoken in the dark.

Chapter Nine

Meeting Michael

Michael at home on California Street in Ashland, Oregon, 1982

My first glimpse of Michael was from behind as he walked in front of me across the Scenic Junior High blacktop on an unusually warm and sunny February day in 1979. I took note of his adorable curly brown hair and cute butt. I had an immediate sense of déjà vu, as if we had met before. In another lifetime maybe? Certainly not in this one. I remembered a conversation I had with Mom in high school when she found me crying in my bedroom because most of the boys were taller than me.

"If your height is a reason they don't want to date you then they are not worth your time," she said. He looked significantly shorter than me. This would be a true test.

How could I be attracted to him when I hadn't even seen his face? I noticed Michael later in the teacher's room surrounded by a bevy of single women fawning over him. He was kind to them but distant and removed. He had wildly curly brown hair, an adorable moustache and warm brown eyes. He looked a lot like me! Several people have told us we look like brother and sister. I found out his name was Michael Jacobvitz and he was an English and auto mechanics teacher, wrestling coach and yearbook advisor, as well as the only single male in the school.

I talked to my guides about him. Was he a good fit for me? What was this sense of knowing him before? I didn't get a specific answer, just a good feeling in my gut, a sense of rightness. I hadn't really pursued a man before and wasn't sure how to go about it.

Should I just walk up to him? What would I say?

The following week, Jack came up to me one day during a break in class.

"Would you like to join our carpool?" he asked. "I know you live in Ashland, and we have room for one more person."

"Sure, that would be great," I said.

I didn't think to ask who the other teachers would be. When I dashed out the front door the next day and into the back seat of the royal blue

Dodge Charger, I was surprised and flustered to be sitting right next to Michael. What were the chances? I came out to Oregon for a job that fell through and then got a job I was not qualified for. It was quite a circuitous route to find the man I was supposed to be with. But the universe doesn't mess around when it wants two people to meet. The carpool was certainly no coincidence.

The "hair picture" circa 1979

I was no longer living with Glenda. The last straw was her telling me I could not cook with garlic because she didn't like the smell. How could one even cook without garlic? That was enough to have me scouring the newspaper for other rentals.

The oak trees in the front yard, black, naked and stripped of their leaves, opened their arms to me as I walked up to the house on Liberty Street in Ashland. The rambling, two-story home had delectable charm with green shutters framing white siding. The moment Luna opened the door chills ran up my arms. I knew this was the right place for me. Luna was a short woman with a pixie haircut and the most loving eyes I had ever seen.

"Welcome!" she said and unlike Glenda I knew she meant it. We wandered through the large, expansive home to a huge backyard and there in the back corner sat a gorgeous, cedar A-frame cabin with a small front porch. Inside to the left was a living room and to the right was a bathroom with a shower. I scrambled up the ladder to see the loft with just enough room for a queen mattress that overlooked the mountains. There was no kitchen. I had to cook on a two-burner electric unit and do my dishes in the shower. The cost was $175 a month.

"I'll take it," I said.

Luna later told me she had many people interested but knew I was the one she wanted to live there. Luna and her family embraced me immediately. She was a single parent of four children.

From day one, I felt like another member of the family. We are still close to this day.

Running down the front steps of Luna's house only a couple of weeks later to join the carpool, I tried not to give away too much when I ended up sitting next to Michael, but a telltale flush appeared on my chest and spread to my face.

"This is Laurie," Jack said from the front seat. "She's a new teacher's aide in my class and also a sign language interpreter for the deaf students."

"I have a couple of deaf students in my auto mechanics class." Michael said.

"I'm only interpreting the easier classes for now until I become more skilled in sign language," I explained. We talked about the logistics of the carpool and conveniently exchanged phone numbers.

A few weeks later, Jack asked me to interpret in Michael's auto mechanics class which was called *Bumps and Curves.* Instantly upon walking into the classroom, I could tell the students loved him. There was a light, jovial atmosphere and they were sincerely having a good time. They were learning how to take apart a lawn mower and put it back together again. They had three tries and if it started, they passed. If it didn't start, they failed. My first day was the day they discovered if all their hard work panned out. My two deaf students, Oliver and Lucas, couldn't hear if it started or not, but they could feel the vibrations. Not that they needed to when they could see the excited response from the other students in the class. I was thrilled when both of their lawn mowers started on the first try. The students called him "Mr. J" and Oliver gave him a sign name that was the letter J carved above the upper lip where Michael had a moustache.

One night a few weeks later, I called Michael to ask him a question about the carpool, and we ended up talking for an hour or two. After that, we called each other regularly and our conversations went on so long that we finally had to stop so we could both have time to sleep. One of our favorite topics was education and how to fix the school system.

Michael believed that teenagers should not sit behind their desks each day and study. "They need to be outside putting all their energy to good use," he said. "They could build homes for people in need, blaze trails in the forest, or work near the ocean learning about marine life."

I thought those were great ideas. "How about teaching them about how to deal with their emotions?" I asked. "The school's solution for dealing with anger or frustration is to send them to the principal's office. That's not too effective."

There was an intimacy to these conversations that left me feeling deeply satisfied. I felt better every time I talked with him; uplifted and filled up.

In late April, my friend Betsy invited me to a party at her house, and I asked Michael to join me. He walked me home and we kissed out in front of my A-frame cottage nestled behind Luna's house under the star-streaked sky. It was electric, just like they talk about in the movies, a perfect dance of lips and tongue. I could feel my heart opening and expanding and other parts of me below my heart as well. I wanted to invite him in, but Henry was driving in to visit me the next day from Eugene. I could envision him walking in on us the next morning. Reluctantly, I separated my body from Michael's and told him I would see him soon. I broke up with Henry that weekend.

Michael cooked gourmet dinners for me on my two-burner hot plate, and we washed the dishes together in the shower. We planted a garden in the small space outside my front porch.

The staff at Scenic were not allowed to date so we had to be discreet. When we spent a weeknight at my place, he would get up early in the morning and run three blocks to his house, change clothes, and walk calmly down the steps to the carpool as though he had slept there all night.

My mother teased me about finding the only single Jew in all of Oregon. There were no synagogues in Ashland in 1979. But Jack was Jewish, and he invited me and Michael over occasionally for Shabbat dinners where we lit the candles to honor the beginning of the Jewish Sabbath at sundown on Friday night just like Mom did at home. Michael's Jewish roots went deep, as did mine, with no interfaith marriages for as many generations back as we could find. I was thrilled to find someone I was so compatible with on so many levels.

Michael and me at a Shabbat dinner at Jack's house.

Michael was born August 31, 1955, in Albuquerque, New Mexico, three weeks to the day after my birth. He was the third of four children, and he credits his father Aaron with teaching him how to write. From a young age, Aaron had Michael write something every day and then would correct it and have him do another draft. It was from these private lessons that Michael honed his writing skills that would serve him well his whole life.

Aaron graduated from Harvard Law School and was a star lawyer at work; his intelligence scored very high on IQ tests. His first date ever was a blind date with Michael's mother, Clara, during his last year of law school. He asked Clara to marry him that night. Clara originally told Aaron no but agreed to the marriage three weeks later. Aaron died three months after our son, Noah, was born in August of 1987. Sadly, our children never got to know him.

Clara and I liked each other immediately and had long conversations, much like Michael and I did, on many different subjects. Clara wanted to be a career woman, and she didn't like being stuck in the traditional role of housewife in the 1950s with four children. Because of that, she encouraged all of her children to work from an early age. Michael got a job at Henry's Hamburgers at 15 years old and has been a hard worker ever since.

After high school, Michael pursued his love of writing and became an English teacher. After his first-year teaching at a high school in Danville, California, he won the Teacher of the Year award for his school district. Three days later, he received a pink slip because he was the last one hired and subsequently found work at Scenic. Without the delivery of that pink slip, he would have slipped away from me.

Marilyn

2003

On June 1, 2003, Laurie called from California. At six feet, Laurie had been awkward, but at 12 she took dancing lessons. She was undaunted when the teacher called her a giraffe. Instead of being cowed, she made the giraffe her symbol. On the other hand, she always tried to please others. Laurie had left for the West Coast at 22 when she graduated from college with a major in counseling and never returned. She had married the only Jewish man she met in Ashland, Oregon. They carpooled to the middle school where they both worked. For a brief time, Laurie sang in a nightclub. They married in Lithia Park in Ashland, Oregon.

Laurie now had a teenage son and daughter. She always baked bread and served gourmet meals. They were wealthy. She and her husband were successful Amway multi-level marketing entrepreneurs on the side. She recently upgraded her interpreting skills, doubling her salary as an interpreter in the schools. She published an article about getting certified after many years of interpreting. She always chauffeured her children, planning their elaborate Bar and Bat Mitzvah celebrations and gave "healings" to her husband Michael when he had knee surgery. Laurie is what is known in the Jewish community as a balabusta.

(Left)

Michael and me at our wedding, August 20, 1983

(Right)

Michael and me singing in the band in the early 1980s

Ashland Daily Tidings in Ashland, Oregon

CHAPTER TEN

Twenty-three Years Later

In August of 2002, I was in the final days of my forty-sixth year. Writing in my journal, I was wondering why the memories came back now. Why did they wait forty-some-odd years to emerge from the murky depths of my subconscious? Why did they decide to come back when I was working day and night and had two children to take care of? How are these things decided?

Twenty-three years ago, I found myself sitting in the back seat of that royal blue Dodge Charger, face to face with Michael, and now I found myself face to face with the ugly memories that had been hidden for so long. I asked my guides why the memories came back now, and they had no answers, but they did tell me I needed to tell Dad. I really didn't want to tell Dad. But following guidance was an important touchstone in my life, so I scheduled a visit back to St. Louis to celebrate my forty-seventh birthday with friends and family---and talk to Dad.

A few weeks later, I climbed to the top of the Cardinals baseball stadium on a blistering hot St. Louis day with Dad and Noah. I was out of breath before we found our seats in the last row all the way to the top. The dust filled my nostrils and the men on the field looked like action figures in a computer game. Noah was 15 years old and a huge baseball fan. He was squirming in his seat, looking all around the stadium, thrilled to be there.

I felt an aching sadness sitting next to Dad knowing my closeness with him was about to end. My thoughts were bouncing around like pinballs in a machine.

- *He is going to die soon so you should just let it go.*

- *No. You must tell him about the horrendous memories.*

- *But I don't want to tell him. It will ruin our relationship.*

- *You need to follow the guides' advice. Oh My God. Don't you understand what happened?! I can't believe you're worried about "ruining your relationship". What an idiot you are!*

- *I must tell him I forgive him. If I tell him I forgive him, everything will get back to normal and we can continue our relationship as it used to be.*

- *Talk to him yes, but how can you forgive him? You just barely found out what happened, and you don't even know all the details.*

My sister Shira threw me a birthday party the following day. I set my fear about talking to Dad aside and enjoyed being with family and friends.

Later that week, I finally got alone time with Dad. We went to a Jewish deli called Blueberry Hill in the Loop, one of my favorite areas in the city with delicious restaurants, shops and movie theatres. The smell of bagels, pastrami, pickles and matzo ball soup greeted us when we walked in the door. I ordered a chopped chicken liver sandwich on tzitzel rye bread with sliced red onions and a dill pickle on the side and we sat in a high-backed wooden booth in the corner. It looked delicious but my stomach felt too jumpy to eat.

After a few minutes of small talk, I blurted out, "You know I'm in therapy and something came up there I want to discuss with you," I said. "I saw images of you touching me in ways that were not okay." I didn't go into detail, and he didn't ask.

"What are you talking about?" he fumed. "I never did any such thing!"

"I want you to know that I forgive you for anything that happened." I said quickly hoping we could just resolve this and move on, and the pain would be over.

"What do you mean?" he said sitting forward in his seat with righteous anger. "There's nothing to forgive. I would never do anything like that!" His words flew toward me filled with rage like a missile aimed straight for my gut.

"Dad," I said, moving back against the wooden booth putting my hands protectively over my mid-section, "I've been in deep emotional and physical pain for a long time. For months, I haven't been able to sleep well, and I've lost my appetite. The memories are visceral and real. There's no way I'm making all this up!"

"I know about False Memory Syndrome," he said cutting me off. "The therapist extracts information under hypnosis that is not true. Roseanne is the daughter of some friends of mine. Her parents got a lawyer and sued the therapist for encouraging Roseanne to make up things about her family. Therapists like to do things like that so they have more problems to deal with and can earn more money."

I sighed. There was no point in trying to convince him. He was adamant. I wondered if he really didn't remember. I felt terrible that I had created this breach between us now. I was angry at my guides for encouraging me to have this conversation and angry at myself for doing it.

Maybe nothing happened. Maybe Dad was right, and I had created false memories. Confused and despondent, I flew back to California with my children.

Mom and me circa 1957

Marilyn

1957

When Laurie, our first daughter, was 16 months old in 1957, we accompanied Bud on his dry goods sales trip to Muncie, Indiana. We had driven in our Chevy with brown fins. It was in a motel there that a doctor came to examine me. He was balding, wore a muted tan business suit and apparently was as ignorant as he was gruff.

He said, "You've caught gonorrhea. You're contagious. Be very careful with the baby. Clean the tub out carefully when you are through or else your daughter will catch your venereal disease."

I felt like a leper. I was horrified. I said to Bud, "Never, ever betray me again!"

He yelled back, "No one tells me what to do! I'll do as I please!"

I was 25, with long brown hair, slim and dimpled. I raced out to the highway and ran down the road, my hair flying behind me, tears staining my cheeks. A man in a black convertible abruptly stopped.

"Child," he said, "things can't be that bad that you are running away from home."

Jolted back to reality, I burst out laughing, "Thanks Sir. I'm all right. I just had a shock. I'm older than I seem."

True to his word, Bud did not stop giving me trichomoniasis and gonorrhea. Looking back at that young woman today, I want to shake her.

What was so frightening? Why couldn't she give up her marriage dream? Why didn't she leave him then? Didn't she know their dissension was damaging their daughter? But, of course, as a typical abuse or incest victim, she always thought it would never happen again.

Chapter Eleven

Dad is Arrested

About a month after I arrived home, I was in the kitchen cooking dinner. I was trying to coordinate the meal, but cooking has never been my strong point. Mushrooms were sautéing in a pan, and marinara sauce was bubbling on the stove. The water was boiling and ready for the spaghetti. Just as I was getting ready to put the spaghetti in the pot, the phone rang. I quickly turned off the burner and answered the phone.

"Hello," I said, breathing a little harder than normal.

"Hi," Shira said. "How are you?" Her voice sounded harried, so I knew it was not good news.

"Fine," I said. "What's wrong?"

"It's Dad," she said "He's been arrested."

"What?" I asked, horrified. "What for?"

"You know how he loves to go swimming," she said. "He organized a game of keep away with some of the kids in the pool." I remembered all too well the sweltering summers in St. Louis. The days spiked to 110 degrees and there were brownouts where they turned off the electricity for hours because too many people were using their air conditioners. For relief, we often went to the neighborhood public swimming pool. Dad would bring a wiffle ball and gather all the children around for a game of keep away. He would throw the ball to one child, and all the other children would try and grab it. Then they would throw it back to him and he would wildly try to find it diving and splashing around in the water. I thought he was just being dramatic.

"There was a young boy there who was playing a game with Dad, and he told the authorities that while Dad was trying to get the ball, he reached down under the water and touched his genitals. The police were called and when they arrived Dad tried to run away. They had to tackle him to the ground."

The black plastic phone receiver was shaking in my hand. "That is awful! Is he okay? Have you talked to him? What does he say happened?"

"Dad was shaken up but not seriously hurt. He told me the boy put the ball in his pocket and was cheating and he was just trying to get the ball out. Dad claims he was totally innocent. He has two charges against him: sexual harassment and resisting arrest."

"What do you think will happen?" I asked. "Do you think Dad is innocent?"

"I don't think he did anything wrong," she said. "It sounds like the boy was exaggerating. They've provided Dad with a public defender. This is his first offense. He should be able to get off."

After I hung up the phone, I could see Dad so eager to get a game of keep away going in the pool. I could see the gleam in his eyes, his fast breathing, his determination to ask other children when one child turned him down, the aggressive way he played the game jumping almost on top of the child to get the ball. He was a man with a mission. A mission that was devastating to innocent young children. Oh my God! Why hadn't I realized what was going on? I thought he just liked children or wanted to have fun. Really, I hadn't thought much about it at all.

The truth hit me like a bullet through my heart. It was searing and unbearable. I sat down in a kitchen chair and forced myself to breathe. One deep breath in. This boy was telling the truth. One deep breath out. Dad was guilty. One deep breath in. I didn't know the truth then. One deep breath out. I know the truth now.

I was shaking. How do I function? It was time to cook dinner and move on with my life. Without consciously deciding my next move, a protective wall came slamming down.

Reading my journal from the fall of 2002, there was no mention of Dad's arrest or how I felt about it. He was arrested! That young boy had the guts to call the authorities and made sure that Dad paid the consequences for his actions. Someone *finally* caught Dad when he was 80 years old! It took long enough. That confirmed what had happened to me. Right? Wrong. I refused to connect what Dad did to that boy in the swimming pool to the memories that were bubbling up to the surface.

For months after Shira's phone call, I had a recurring dream. Michael, Noah and I were in a hotel, and we had a dead body to get rid of. We nervously took the body in the elevator down to the basement, but the elevator doors wouldn't open. Michael told me I killed this person, but I didn't remember killing anyone. Then I had a flashback, a brief memory of killing someone. It switched to another scene in the hotel where we were still trying to offload the body to no avail. After what seemed like hours, I woke up terrified but relieved that I had not really killed anyone. My subconscious could not pierce through my denial.

Eight months later, I was listening to a tape by Oriah Mountain Dreamer sitting on a chair in my living room with the sun pouring through the window when she read this poem:

<u>The True Names of Birds</u>
by Sue Goyette

There are more ways to abandon a child
than to leave them at the mouth of the woods.
Sometimes by the time you find them, they've made up names
for all the birds and constellations, and they've broken
their reflections in the lake with sticks.

With my daughter came promises and vows
that unfolded through time like a road map and led me
to myself as a child, filled with wonder for my father
who could make sound from a wide blade of grass

and his breath. Here in the stillness of forest,
the sun columning before me temple-ancient,
that wonder is what I regret losing most; that wonder
and the true names of birds.

Printed with permission of the author;
From the book: <u>The True Names of Birds</u>
1998 (eighth printing 2022) by Brick Books

I started to bawl; loud gasping sounds came pouring from my mouth like gun bursts. Tears cascaded down my face and snot came out of my nose. After what felt like hours of crying, but was probably only minutes, the image of Little Laurie unfurled in my mind's eye. I could see her clearly with goopy black gook glommed onto her dancing brown curls. Piercing hazel eyes inside deep dark sockets latched onto mine within a face etched with pain. I gasped with surprise and delight. She was here. She had come back to me, rising out of that black goop. My tears stopped. I blew my nose. I looked at her with rapt attention.

"You know now," she told me. "Dad hurt me, he scared me, he did horrible, unmentionable things to me. It was not just me. He violated the boy in the swimming pool and many, many other children."

"I believe you," I said. "What can I do to help?"

"Listen to me," she said. "I have many things I want to tell you."

"I will," I said. "I promise."

It was time for the truth to be unveiled.

Marilyn

2002

So, despite my college degree, I was uneducated, and did not recognize the signs of sexual abuse in my own home. I was upset in the fall of 2002 to hear that Bud, the children's father, had been arrested for child molestation in the YMCA swimming pool.

He said, which I am sure he believed, that it was an entirely accidental touching in the middle of a "game".

Chapter Twelve

Dead Bear, Dead Dad

I am on the right with Dad circa 1960

The next day, I carved out some time alone and went into my office. It was in the back of the house on the first floor with sea green walls and carpet to match. I settled comfortably into my padded folding chair in front of my altar. On my altar were fresh sage, candles, and rocks of many shapes and sizes including my "forgiveness stone" which was a small, flat, green and white stone I found online that carries the energy of forgiveness inside of it. I grasped it tightly to help me get through whatever my inner child had to tell me. The first thing I saw after closing my eyes and using some of the techniques I learned in therapy was Little Laurie climbing up into my lap. She told me she had some things to show me.

There were two different scenes:

1. *I was a baby crying and Mom threw me up against the wall and screamed at me to shut up.*

2. *I was 2 or 3 years old and sitting at the dinner table with Mom and Dad. Mom screamed at Dad and he shoved the food off the table. Then, when he left, she shook me and screamed at me. I was frozen in shock.*

Every day I made time to be with Little Laurie, listen to her and watch what she wanted me to see. It was such a visceral feeling for me to see myself so young and feel my terror and powerlessness. There were similar memories that came up with Mom for the whole week. It was searingly painful to watch but I had promised Little Laurie, and I would not let her down.

The following week Little Laurie was mostly out of the black gook that she was immersed in when I first contacted her in therapy. She still had a little bit in her hair and on her clothes. I took some time with her to wash her hair in a basin. Most of the gook came off.

She sat on my lap, and we hugged for a while and then she pulled open this curtain. Behind that was another curtain and there was only blackness. As I watched, I slowly saw another image of Little Laurie coming into view.

She was crying. It was like a movie within a movie. The Little Laurie on my lap was watching the Little Laurie behind the curtain with me.

I asked her why she was crying, and this huge monster head came out from her body. It was putrid green with jagged teeth. When he opened his mouth to growl, drool dripped down his jaw. The Little Laurie on my lap was frightened, and I reassured her that I would protect her. The Little Laurie in the movie kept disappearing inside the monster and then she would come back out. Finally, she came up out of the monster and stayed there and I asked her to show us what happened.

> *I was about 5 years old, had wet my pants in the middle of the night and went into my parents' bedroom. Dad woke up and went into the bathroom with me to help me change into dry clothes. He took off my pajamas and started touching me all over my body. Then he rubbed against me with his erection. He told me to take his penis and put it in my mouth. I tried, but I started crying and said it was too big. He spanked me for not doing a good job. When I started crying, he masturbated in front of me. He put me back in bed with no clothes on and told me what a bad girl I was. The curtains closed.*

I held Little Laurie in my lap. She clung to me and cried. I was so angry, I was shaking. I reminded myself that my inner child was my priority.

"I am all grown up now," I said. "I will keep you safe." She stayed on my lap, and we hugged for a long time. I was fiercely protective of her and determined not to let her down. Most importantly, I finally believed her, and no one was ever going to convince me otherwise.

The next day she told me more about that experience. "After what happened in the bathroom with Dad, I was scared all the time," she said. "Every time Mom left, I was scared that Dad would do something bad to me again. I was also scared to use the bathroom in the middle of the night, so I wet the bed until I was about 9 years old. I was so terrified I didn't know if I wanted to live anymore. That was when I became sick and went to the hospital. I was there for a long time and almost died."

Mom had told me I missed six months of kindergarten because I had chicken pox followed by measles and then pneumonia. I could see how it would be impossible living each day with those feelings of fear swamping me. I had to find a way to cope. Thank goodness I survived and have created a wonderful life with a great career and a husband and two children whom I love dearly.

"When I finally went back to school for first grade," Little Laurie continued, "they put me in the 'slow' class for children who had behavior problems. Mom went to the principal and fought for me to be put back in the regular first grade classroom."

"Yes," I said. "Mom told me that story more than once. It was good that she fought for me."

That same year, 1961, my brother was born. The day Ben was born and my parents brought him home, I ran the whole way from school three blocks downhill past the huge oak trees to see him. I stopped and panted, hands on my knees, as I arrived at the red brick walkway to our front door. Ben was in the living room lying in a wooden cradle. He had thick black hair all over his head and looked so cute. I leaned over the cradle and whispered in his ear, "I promise I will protect you from Daddy and Mommy."

Back in my office, Little Laurie opened the curtain to show me one more scene.

One night, Mom was gone and the three of us were at home alone with Dad. It was shortly after Ben was born. I was 6 years old, and Shira was 3 years old. Ben was sleeping in his cradle in the children's bedroom and Shira and I were with Dad in his bedroom across the hall. The bed looked huge and took up most of the small room.

Dad said, "Let's play Dead Bear."

"No!" I screamed, starting to cry.

He grabbed me and laid on top of me, forcing me down on the bed. It was Shira's job to see if she could pull him off me.

"I'm too heavy," he said growling. "A dead bear." I was terrified and furious and squirmed under him to his delight. I could feel something sharp and hard poking at my stomach. Shira tried to pry his body off me to no avail. I screamed at him "Get off me!" and pummeled him with my small fists with all my might. Finally, after what seemed like an eternity, he stood up.

I jumped up and screamed at Shira "Go back to your room!" She looked at me with huge brown eyes and shook her head no.

I took her by her shoulders looking right at her. "Please go," I said softly.

She left and I was standing in the hall between the two rooms with Dad. I looked way up at his tall, towering form. His rumpled pajama bottoms were sticking out funny. "No more Dead Bear," I said with a firm voice. "No more touching me in places that feel yucky and the same thing with Shira. Don't you dare!" My voice was low, but clear. I shook my small finger at him, my face scrunched up with rage.

"I hate Dead Bear. If you ever try to do it to me or her again, I will kill you!"

Dad stood there with a confused look on his face. I went into my bedroom and slammed the door. He did not follow me.

As I watched the scene, I was deeply moved by my bravery. I know now I was too young to protect my siblings but at the time I could feel that my need to protect them was enormous. I didn't care about the size difference or the inadequacy of my threat.

"Was he scared? Did my threat make a difference?" I asked Little Laurie.

"Yes. It pretty much stopped after that. You forgot. But *I didn't forget.*"

"No, you didn't forget. It is important that you remember what happened," I reassured her. "I need you to remember because those painful memories will always be a part of who I am."

"Why didn't you tell someone like Mom or our grandmothers?" I asked her.

"I didn't want to leave my family. I knew if I told someone they would come and take me away and no matter how awful things were, I didn't want to go."

"I understand," I said. "I love you." I gave her a huge hug.

Marilyn

2003

There may be many who saw the movie "Capturing the Friedmans" primarily for an artistic impression, but there are those of us who went to understand the patterns, the clues to incest and pedophilia that occurred in our own lives. Impressions that were not apparent to us at the time. I saw the movie just two weeks after I heard the news that changed my view of marriage. I was in Brooklyn visiting my cousin. She suggested we see the movie. I did not object.

I wasn't prepared, however, for what I saw. I sobbed through "Capturing the Friedmans". I continually had these "aha" experiences from what I saw on the screen. Being married but avoiding your wife, capturing the children to the exclusion of your spouse, and playing games. In our house, it was "dead bear", the father flopping on his children, despite their screams of protest, an erection happening and keeping the sadistic pornography magazines not totally hidden in the closet. (At the time I did not know an erection was happening). Denial as they, the incestuous, pedophilia fathers are as out of body, as unconscious of what they do, as the abused children who leave their bodies to survive.

Chapter Thirteen

Dad is Convicted

The dam had burst open now and memories came pouring forth. They would force their way into my consciousness like acid eating through metal. Every day the poison would crawl out of my brain spilling into my life like molten lava making its way through the earth's crust. The emotional anguish was overwhelming.

The memories were relentless. They came through in the tub, walking down the street, at night when I got up to pee, and sitting at my desk. I never knew when they would strike next. The reverberations permeated my body like electric shocks. The constant zapping was debilitating. I was exhausted, walking through my life like a zombie. "It wouldn't be happening if you couldn't handle it," my guides told me when I complained to them it was too much.

(from Laurie's journal, 2003)

May 5, 2003

Ken, my craniosacral therapist, was helping me with pain in my hip. While he was working on me, we called in my guides and did this visualization where I saw a screw going from my hip down to my ankle. I unscrewed it, took it out and it was all bloody. I threw it in the trash. There was a gaping wound in my leg. My guides filled it with light, but it was still there. Later, when I was in the bath, I saw the wound again and this memory came up:

> *I was home alone with Dad. He was mad at me because I didn't eat all the food on my plate. He chased me under the table. He pulled down my underwear and spanked me and fondled my vagina while he jacked off. After that, he left. I stayed under the table and tried to become small enough so I could disappear. It didn't work. I cried for a long time before I fell asleep.*

Afterwards, I was disgusted and nauseous. I fell into bed.

May 6, 2003

> *I was out in the hall with Dad and he was mad I was going to bed late. He pulled down my pajamas and spanked me and fondled me. He held me up in the air and I threw up. He was grossed out and dropped me. I landed in the vomit. He left. I ran into the bathroom and curled in a ball in the back of the*

tub. I didn't wash off the vomit. After a long time, I washed my face and ran into bed.

May 7, 2003

I peed on the floor. Dad found me and started to spank me. I screamed for Mom to help me. She came out of the bedroom. Dad let go and I ran to my room and hid under the covers curled into a ball. Mom told me not to worry about the pee on the floor. "It can happen to anyone," she said.

Why would Dad do these things to his own child? Didn't he have any feelings of remorse? I was so disgusted! Little Laurie was so small and vulnerable. My feelings of pain and outrage cycled through me night and day. The repercussions continued to infiltrate my life.

Then, for a blessed ten days the memories stopped. I basked in the peacefulness of the break as I was steeling myself for the next one to pop up. On Sunday May 18, 2003, Shira called again. I was in the kitchen making a birthday cake for Noah's sixteenth birthday. "Dad's trial was yesterday," she said. "He was convicted of sexual molestation and sentenced to eight months in jail. He had a public defender who did a lousy job. Dad is going to appeal and wanted me to ask you for a character reference to help his case."

I sat there in silence, terrified to say anything. I couldn't believe this was happening to me.

"Let me call you back," I finally said.

There was no way I could provide a character reference. But, it felt too soon to share the memories with my family. What explanation could I give my sister? While I was panicking, I also felt a sense of relief and deep satisfaction that Dad was *finally* convicted. I called Paul, my therapist, and left a message. I tried to call Michael who was out preparing for Noah's birthday party at the park, but he didn't answer his phone. I called the sexual abuse hotline in desperation.

"You have to tell her the truth," they told me. "You have no choice." Both Paul and Michael called me back and told me the same thing.

I finished putting the chocolate icing on the yellow cake with shaking hands, got out the candles, took a deep breath and made the call. It was one of the hardest things I had ever done in my life. "I've been thinking about your request, and I can't write the reference," I blurted out with no preamble when Shira answered the phone.

"Why not?" she asked. I could hear the frustration in her voice. I knew she was wondering why I wouldn't comply with this one simple request.

"Because memories have been coming up to the surface about things Dad did to me when I was young." Each word was a tremendous effort to say like pounding a nail through a piece of hardwood.

"Really? What happened?"

"He touched me and did things to me that are unacceptable," I said. I shared some examples with her.

"Okay," she said totally avoiding the bombshell I had just dropped in her lap. "I'll let Dad know you won't write one. They also insisted that Dad go to a psychiatrist, and he was diagnosed with bipolar disorder. He refused to accept the diagnosis or the medication."

Bipolar disorder. Mental illness. I felt like a top spinning endlessly with no place to land. Could this be one reason why Dad was a pedophile? His mental illness?

Many years later, after Dad had passed, Shira told me Dad never asked *her* for a character reference, only *me.* She was wondering why. I told her about the conversation I had with Dad at the deli before his arrest at the swimming pool where I told Dad about the memories coming back. We both realized he was asking me for a character reference because he was worried that I was going to fly out to St. Louis for the trial and testify against him. He didn't want to ask me directly, so he had Shira be the intermediary.

Shira was not expecting to be hit by this news of sexual abuse in our family. I can only imagine the shock for her and the burden of having to deal with this situation in St. Louis alone, but at the time I wasn't thinking about anyone but me.

That night in the tub, I felt pain under my left shoulder blade and this memory emerged:

> *We had a whole grove of trees behind our home where I loved to play. Dad came out and found me there. He started "play wrestling" with me. We fell to the ground, and he put his hands under my clothes. I was crying and screaming for help, but we were too far from the house. A rock lodged under my left shoulder blade. Dad got up and I rolled over, grabbed the small rock and threw it at him. It only made a glancing blow off his side but it still gave me a small sense of satisfaction. I decided*

not to go out in the forest behind our yard again because it wasn't safe. That was one of my favorite places in nature and I was angry at Dad for taking that away from me.

The next morning, I went to the DMV with Noah so he could take the driver's test. I felt a deep sense of sadness when I saw him drive away. It was one more indication that he was leaving me, becoming independent and moving out into the world.

That afternoon in therapy during EMDR, I saw the following image:

Little Laurie grew big and flipped Dad in a karate move. Then she stabbed him and killed him. She was dancing joyfully after he died. She started crying and told me: "I wanted to do those things to Dad in real life, but I wasn't big enough."

The scene changed to Little Laurie crying on the back porch of our house around 5 years old. She was feverish, delirious and alone on her cot. "If I can't kill Dad, then I want to die," she pleaded. "Please let me die!"

Several angels surrounded by white light showed up in front of her. One angel came towards Little Laurie, her whole body glowing aqua blue with huge gossamer wings trailing out behind her. Little Laurie dried her eyes and sat up mesmerized by her beauty.

"I am your guardian angel," she said. "It's not time for you to die. We are all here to help you forget the awful things that

happened. When you forget, you will not be able to see us again because it will bring back the memories."

My Guardian Angel, Mariah, turned to talk with me, the adult Laurie. "Now I can be in your life again," she said with a big smile. "Just ask for me and I will come to you."

I was grateful to have Mariah back in my life. Now it was time to tell Mom the truth.

Marilyn

2003

Referring to the fact that her father had been arrested for child molestation last fall in the YMCA swimming pool and would be tried in a few weeks, I said, "Do you know that Dad physically tortured your brother by squeezing his knees until he was 24? Ben said the pain was so exquisite, it felt like hitting your crazy bone. Dad would laugh, however, when Ben screamed for him to stop."

Laurie said, "Mom, do you think Ben was the only one?"

I was in the kitchen preparing a salmon souffle for a birthday lunch for friends. While I talked, I scraped carrots.

Laurie continued, "Why do you think I wet my bed at night until I was nine? Why do you think I changed from an angel to a hellion at three? Why do you think I was so dazed in kindergarten that the teachers thought I was dumb? Why do you think I nearly died at six? Dad came in at night. He fingered me. He told me I was a bad daughter as he did it. My urine burned. I cried. Didn't you hear me? Where were you? And you call yourself 'the mother in charge of health and safety'? And you yelled at me when Dad got angry with you? Why did you ever marry him?

Why didn't you leave him?"

I put down my carrot peeler. Through my sobs I said, "Laurie, I never knew. I am so sorry it ever happened. I am so sorry I did not do more."

Chapter Fourteen

Telling Mom

"Hi Mom," I said, when she answered the phone. "With Dad's trial and incarceration happening, I wanted to let you know why I didn't send in a letter vouching for his good character. I have been having some memories come through about what happened with Dad and with you when I was young."

I talked about the basics of what happened: physical, sexual and emotional abuse. When I got to the part about where I wanted to die, she started to cry.

"Oh my God," she said. "I had no idea that was happening with you and Dad!"

"Do you believe me?" I asked.

"Yes, I do," she said. "Dad had some issues. Things were really challenging with him and me from the beginning. I thought about leaving him when you were about 16 months old, but in the 1950s a single mother had nowhere to go. No woman left her husband back then because we had no way to support ourselves."

Finally, someone believed me! At the same time, I was not letting her off the hook.

"I am glad you believe me," I said. "It means a lot. But you were no saint either, screaming at me like that."

"I know I made it worse by taking my anger out on you. You were so small and that was the wrong thing to do," she said, her voice full of anguish. I was not ready to hear her apology.

"I am angry right now and I need some space to work things out. I wanted to get back to you and let you know what was happening with me and why I refused to write the affidavit."

"I understand, Laurie. Take the time that you need. I'm sorry, so sorry for everything."

I wondered what she meant by Dad had some "issues." I had so many questions for her, but I was too worn out and overwhelmed to ask. I needed time to breathe and regroup. A few days later Shira called again.

"Dad got out of the eight-month jail sentence. He is only going to jail for two weekends."

I got a deep sense of satisfaction out of some punishment being meted out. But two weekends for everything that happened to me, and God knows who else still didn't feel like enough. On the other hand, what was enough? What would it take to make him stop being a pedophile?

"He did have to register as a sexual offender," she went on to say. "They took his picture and put it up on the website."

Good. I wanted the whole world to know.

"Did you believe me when I told you what happened?" I asked her. It took all my courage to ask, and I cowered waiting for the answer.

"I am angry you told Mom. Now Mom will tell the whole town! You know how she is. I don't want people to know. You were way too graphic when you told me what happened. It really upset me."

"I'm sorry," I said, and immediately regretted saying it. My sister intimidated me, and apologizing had become my rote response. It felt like I was constantly apologizing to her, and I resented that. Why should I be sorry? I hadn't done anything wrong. Telling Mom was my right. Shira still had not answered my question. Did she believe me or not? I was having a hard time breathing and could feel my anger rising up in me like a coiled snake ready to strike.

"I can't take care of you and deal with everything here as the only child in St. Louis. You need too much from me right now," she said. She was blaming me, but this was not my fault! Why was I the one being blamed?

Suddenly, I was done. It was too much dealing with the pain of the memories coming back and having conflict with my sister. "I guess there is nothing more to say. I will leave you alone. Goodbye." I hung up before I said something I would regret.

Later in the day, I took some time out to be with Little Laurie. I closed my eyes and visualized myself as a little child. She told me she wanted to show me some things about Shira when we were young.

> *We were playing in the backyard in our childhood home. I was around 6 years old and Shira about 3 years old. Dad came stomping outside, furious about something. He started hitting Shira and I tried to protect her.*
>
> *STOP!" I yelled. I pounded on his back with my little fists, but I was so small, and he was too big. I started crying. In the second scene, I was bouncing a big red ball in our backyard.*
>
> *Shira asked me, "What should we do about Dad?" I kept bouncing the ball. I was the oldest. I was in charge. I was*

responsible. Should we run away? Where would we go? I was confused and angry with myself that I didn't have a solution.

"I don't know," I told her.

What else happened to Shira? How bad did it get for her? I was not asking her about that now, but I wondered, nonetheless.

How about Ben? I knew I was too young to do anything when this happened, but deep in my heart, as the eldest child, I felt responsible for both of my siblings. Guilt gnawed at me deep inside like a ravenous rat. I knew I had failed them.

Shira and I were in too much pain to be there for each other, to empathize and get a true sense of what each other's lives were like. Both of us wanted that sisterly connection, but like trapeze artists grasping for the swing and missing, it felt just out of reach.

After my session with Little Laurie, I looked online at the sexual offender website and found Dad's picture with his name underneath: Bernard B. Goodman. A tremendous sense of rightness filled my being and for a moment took away the searing pain. There it was in black and white, the truth.

Marilyn

2003

For the first time I wished I had never married Bud. I would always think that without marrying him, I would not have had such wonderful children. But now, I thought I had done them a great disservice at least by staying married and by yelling and occasionally hitting my children. I had been dazed as I dealt with a crazed man. I had moved from my parent's home to my spouses house. I knew too little about life.

Bud, however, was a sensitive and iconoclastic man who had been repressed. He was the first Reform Jewish boy to be Bar Mitzvahed in St. Louis. Hitler had come to power, but he was not yet a world menace. Bud had written a pacifist speech that the rabbis rejected. He needed to deliver a different teaching, Later, despite his pacifist leanings, he became a world killer in the 1940's. In World War II, he climbed the mountains in Italy in the United States defense and was decorated as a war hero for rescuing his fellow soldiers. Under his eyes, the shrapnel remained like dark slate.

Chapter Fifteen

Candace

Tomorrow, and tomorrow, and tomorrow,
Creeps in this petty pace from day to day,
To the last syllable of recorded time;
And all our yesterdays have lighted fools
The way to dusty death.
Out, out, brief candle!
Life's but a walking shadow, a poor player,
That struts and frets his hour upon the stage,
And then is heard no more. It is a tale
Told by an idiot, full of sound and fury,
Signifying nothing.

—Shakespeare's Macbeth Act 5 Scene 5

My name at birth was Laurie Candace Goodman. Dad told me he named me Candace after the character 'Candace Compson' in the book '*The Sound and The Fury*' by William Faulkner, one of his favorite authors. I never liked my middle name. When I married Michael, my maiden name became my middle name, Laurie Goodman Jacobvitz. Candace was gone, dismissed, never to be heard of again. Except, was she?

Published in 1929, *The Sound and the Fury* is set in Jefferson, Mississippi in the first third of the twentieth century. Much like the passage in Macbeth it is named after, the story is a tragedy. Of the four children, Candace is the only girl. Her brothers Benjy and Quentin both adore her. Benjy is developmentally disabled. After he attacks a young girl, he is committed to a local asylum and castrated there. Quentin commits suicide in his 20s. After the father dies, the last son, Jason, who is a racist and responsible for terrible treatment of Benjy, leads the family to financial ruin.

Candace, according to Faulkner, is the hero of the story. She is sexually promiscuous, gets pregnant and then marries someone else. When her husband finds out the child is not his, he kicks her out. She moves back in with her daughter, Jason and her mom.

When her daughter grows up and runs away from home, Candace goes to Paris where she lives with a German general during the occupation.

Even though I didn't like the name, and I like the story even less, I am still curious about why Dad gave me the name Candace. The Compson family and our family were both dysfunctional. But I think there is a deeper connection. Faulkner was fascinated with the theme of intergenerational trauma in the families of both the southern Whites who were the perpetrators and the southern Blacks who were the victims. Intergenerational trauma was a theme for our family as well. Did Dad know that? Did he see the connection?

I wasn't even thinking about my ancestors when I decided to go on a river cruise with Michael in the summer of 2016. We got a good deal on a Viking cruise called *The Danube Waltz* and flew to Budapest. I knew our ancestors were from Eastern Europe but had never really been drawn to go there. I thought France, Spain and Italy were the places to go because they were more popular. I was guessing Eastern Europe was probably not as nice. Maybe that was part of the reason why my ancestors left. I was wrong.

Budapest was one of the most beautiful places I had ever seen. We had made the rookie traveling mistake of not arriving early, so we didn't have much time to see the city. Deciding to take a walk early the next morning, we sauntered down the embankment following the Danube River and came to a sculpture called *The Shoes on the Danube Bank.* It was a memorial erected in 2005 to honor the Jews who were asked to take off their shoes (because they were valuable) and then were shot and killed in 1944-45 by fascist Hungarian militia and subsequently tossed in the river.

I was drawn in, crouching down by the shoes, totally riveted by the sculpture. I could feel the spirits of my ancestors there. By ancestors, I don't mean only my family ancestors, but also the Jews because the Jews are my tribe. It was a visceral feeling that snaked its way up my arms and legs and speared my soul. I was kneeling, tears staining my cheeks, when I started talking to them as if they were there in flesh and blood. I told them how sorry I was they had to go through that violent death. Their energy was so strong that when our boat took off later that night, I could still sense their silent shadows hovering along the bank as we passed by.

The Shoes on the Danube Bank sculpture in Budapest — Artists: Can Togay and Gyula Pauer

The beauty of Austria and Slovakia as we floated through castles and charming countryside felt like something out of a perfect painting. We left the boat to explore the small towns in the sparkling sunshine, perusing the shops, eating delicious pastries and enjoying the spectacular views. In Passau, Germany, we took a bus to Prague, Czech Republic, and it was there that we went to the Jewish Museum which had hundreds of items confiscated from the Jews during the war that were never returned because the owners were either killed or decided not to come back to Prague.

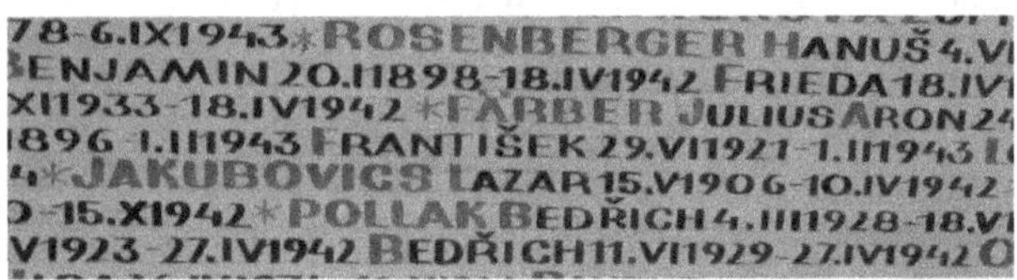

Jacobvitz ancestor on the wall in the Prague Holocaust Museum

The most chilling and disturbing exhibit was in the Pinkas Synagogue where more than 80,000 names of Holocaust victims were meticulously written on the walls. We looked for people with our surnames Rubin (for Michael's mom) and Probe (for my mom). There was Dad's last name which was Guttmen before they changed it to the more Americanized,

Goodman. But by far, the name we found the most was a variation of our last name: Jacobovich, Jacobowitz or Jakubovics. There were literally hundreds of them. It was profoundly heartbreaking to see all those lives that were lost, all those people who had plans and goals and never had a chance to live their full life.

Jews have been persecuted for centuries. Many people believe the holocaust was the culmination of Judenhass or Jew hate.

How had this trauma pervaded my family? I only have snippets of knowledge. Mom hinted she had been abused giving no specific details. I knew that Grandma Lillian's Mom had been sent to an insane asylum after the store she and her husband owned went out of business.

There are so many questions I don't have answers to. How prevalent was mental illness in the generations before me? How was Dad affected by fighting in the war? How were my ancestors affected by living through the Holocaust? How was Mom abused? The truth about my family is hazy with holes that will probably never be filled like cigarette burns on a lace tablecloth. Regardless, there was enough upheaval, confusion and damage to cause great anguish.

What are the effects of intergenerational trauma? How do we stop passing it down? Healing myself by unveiling the truth is what I believe works. As I heal myself, I heal my children and my ancestors.

Even though we both have dysfunctional families, Candace's life was a tragedy. Mine is not. Candace is no longer a part of my name.

Mother's Quilt

By Marilyn Probe

March 31, 2008

My mother passes her appliqué guilt to me,
all affection laundered out of it to keep
its true colors in my heart. She never cradles
my cheeks in the crook of her knees,

but slips her image into mine,
her open at the throat brown blouse,
her hair in supple waves, fluid movements,
magical hands. She is fully three dimensional

like a ring patterned quilt, sculpted. I inherited her calm,
anxiety, anger and though she did not consistently
support me in life, now her love buoys me each day.
After she died, she came in dreams, I could almost touch.

Mother is synthesized within me as I strive to drop her anger.
*I can hear her saying—**rage has left me and it can leave you.***

CHAPTER SIXTEEN

Raining Yellow Jackets

During all the emotional pain and working day and night that Spring of 2003, Michael and I decided to add another spinning plate to our lives. We both hated the master bathroom design where the toilet was the star attraction with only one sink right in front of it. But we especially hated the tub. It was a rectangular Roman tub with dingy white tiles we could never get clean. When I leaned back in the bath, the sharp corners poked me in the back. I tried buying a plastic bath pillow with suction cups, but it kept falling off. When the planter box in the tub started leaking, the plumber said we had dry rot. We were more than ready to remodel as we bought the house "as is."

What started out as a bathroom project soon spiraled out of control. We fixed the dry rot that went all the way down the south side of the house, scraped the popcorn off the ceilings and added lighting, tore up the old carpet, got new cabinets and flooring in the kitchen, and discovered electrical issues that were not up to code.

I had been reading about feng shui and decided to hire an expert to come to our home. Feng shui is a Chinese system that arranges things in your environment so that they are in harmony and balance with the natural world around you to create more love, wealth, and health. The woman I hired was small and thin with an angular face and kind smile. She arrived one Saturday morning in early May when Michael was out of town for work and gave me suggestions for changes in our home such as putting a mirror in my office so I could see the door behind me as I sat at my desk, and rounding the corners of the walls. Afterwards, she burned some herbs wrapped in tinfoil on the stove doing an incantation in Chinese to clear the house of any negative energy. They smelled pungent, but not unpleasant.

After she was done, I went upstairs to put on business clothes for my Amway meeting that afternoon, high heels and a flouncy lavender dress that came to mid-thigh. I walked delicately down the stairs over a drop cloth to our living room. To my horror, I noticed yellow jackets were pouring in through both living room windows.

Whacking away at the yellow jackets with a fly swatter, my lavender dress twirling around me, I yelled up the stairs to Noah and Rachel "Call pest control!" The yellow jackets seemed drunk on some fancy liqueur as they dropped through the window frame like coins through a slot machine struggling to get upright after they fell.

"Leave-go-shoo!" I screamed at them. Why was Michael always out of town when a crisis happened?

After making several calls, Rachel finally got a pest control worker to come out on the weekend for an extra fee. He found the yellow jacket nest on the north side and sprayed some chemicals inside. The yellow jackets stopped coming in the house leaving their carcasses littering the windowsill and living room floor like yellow shrapnel from a fragmentation grenade.

Later, I remembered the feng shui ceremony and wondered if there could be a connection. I called the woman, and she told me the north section of the house represents children and family, and the yellow jackets represent anger. At first, I was mad at having this crisis happen because I decided to have a feng shui expert come to my house. But later, I realized the yellow jackets were such a good symbol for me. Their house invasion with stinging energy was a good metaphor for the painful memories and the dead yellow jackets were memories that had been exhumed and put to rest. There was a sense of satisfaction with that. My home space had been defended, and we were healing together.

The last thing I felt like doing that afternoon was going to an Amway meeting. I was totally discombobulated, my nerves frazzled, but I forced myself into the car. Our venue had recently changed from a spacious 400-person auditorium with comfortable cushioned chairs to a small, windowless room with 200 flimsy metal folding chairs. Losing people in the Amway business is common but the hope is you can add people at the same time, so it won't be noticeable.

There was an enormous fireplace up front with pasty yellow brick and a lime green iron awning in the middle. Four circular matching lime green chandeliers with fleur de lis on both sides hung over us in the middle of the room like UFOs waiting to take flight. The smell of mildew from the stained, worn-out brown carpet permeated the air. The side doors were open to let in a breeze but there was no wind, and the room was oppressively hot.

I was working at the ticket table with motivational materials for sale as people walked in. "*Let's Get It Started In Here,*" by the Black-Eyed Peas blasted from the speakers. Amid the smiles, there was a feeling of awkwardness and embarrassment among the leadership that our numbers were shrinking. Sitting with me at the table was Charlotte, a woman with cascading blonde hair and a ready smile. She and her husband Luke were Mormon, staunch Republicans, and the leaders of our local group. Despite our religious and political differences, Charlotte and I found common ground as mothers of young children. I had two teenagers and welcomed her advice and the respite from listening to another meeting.

In the larger auditorium, the ticket table was located outside in the foyer so Charlotte and I could communicate easily without distracting the audience. But now, we had to surreptitiously whisper to each other. I also scurried around the audience handling logistics like giving people the right change or items they had forgotten to pick up, relieved to have something to do.

After Luke gave a speech and introduced our guest speakers for the afternoon, he came back to the table and motioned for me to follow him out into the empty lobby. He loomed over me like a large yellow jacket, his blonde hair sticking up and long limbs curled in like he was getting ready for the sting.

"You need to listen when I talk on stage," he said, his voice low and tight. "You are setting a bad example for the team."

"It's really hard," I said, a red blush seeping up my neck. "I've heard those same stories repeatedly."

"Well gut up and listen to them one more time," he snapped.

"That's part of your job."

I wanted to kick him in the balls, but instead I just nodded. As I went back into the room, it felt like I was walking into a prison cell, stifling and confined.

A few months later, I was at Adel's restaurant in Santa Rosa eating with the people in our Amway business after a meeting. We took over the back room of the restaurant, each business group eating together at tables. Michael and I both loved to socialize, grabbing a club sandwich with French fries or a hot fudge sundae while chatting with our business partners at the different tables. This was my favorite part of the night.

At the end of the night, we walked out the door with Luke and Charlotte into the familiar parking lot. The rank smell of garbage emanated from the back of the building and there were hundreds of cigarette butts scattered on the black top like white splats of paint on a black canvas. While Charlotte and Michael were talking, Luke turned his back to them and faced me. He bent over me, his face stern.

"Someone in your group told me you are not going to the SAM event," he said glowering down at me.

The Skin Analyzer Machine (SAM) was a marketing tool we used to show women where their skin was damaged. The customer put their heads through a small opening, and an Amway distributor looked through a window on the opposite side. The UV light showed the imperfections on their skin and then recommendations were given of specific Amway products that would help. I was keenly aware that Luke and Charlotte were earning money from this event.

That's right. I'm not planning to go." I looked up at him defiantly.

"Charlotte is taking time out of her life to attend and as a leader, I expect you to be there."

"It's not laziness," I replied. "I was abused by my father and being in an enclosed space like the SAM is scary for me." I was surprised to hear the words come out of my mouth. My eyes teared up as I said it and I realized how hard it was to hold all of this in and what a relief it was to tell someone, anyone.

"I don't care what your excuse is. I expect you to be there," he quipped without losing a beat.

Even though Luke and I had a tumultuous relationship, I was expecting some compassion. When I got none, it was a shock. His response felt like he was grinding his heel into my heart. I didn't consciously choose to tell Luke, of all people, but when he unleashed his anger on me, my pain came exploding out of me like a runaway train. When he took me aside at the Amway event earlier that year, I wasn't ready to confront him. But now I was letting my truth come to the surface after years of repression. Despite the intense pain and the messiness of the circumstances, it felt empowering to let Little Laurie's voice be heard.

Marilyn

1978

I never assessed Buddy as mentally ill, not even when he ran a prostitution ring that he called an Escort Service. Bud had been so down, barely able to get out of bed after his own business failed. When his father's business closed, Bud set up his own dry goods business in our cherry paneled study. I was his business manager and set up the firm with staff in our home. Despite the cigar smoke, I wanted to get closer to Bud.

He probably felt smothered. Although today, remarried, Bud has told more than one friend, "Marilyn and I had a perfect marriage. She was my greatest love."

Bud in his next business, with his imaginative mind, listed sexy sayings in the Yellow Pages as metaphors that brought in a huge response. He housed the women "escorts" in an apartment building that he rented. The women got into brawls and tore the sinks off the walls. He lost $10,000 in the venture.

One day I got a call from someone who said he had connections to the mafia.

"May I speak to Mrs. Goodman?" he asked,

"This is she," I said.

I wasn't so cautious in those days in checking first as to who was calling.

He continued, "If your husband doesn't return the girls' property immediately, we'll kill your son."

Chapter Seventeen

Telling Dad

At the end of June 2003, I was driving home when I heard my cell phone ring and saw on the caller ID that it was my sister calling. My stomach dropped with nervous anticipation. I pulled over to the side of the road next to an empty field with waving strands of amber grass.

"Hello," I said, my heart in my throat.

"Hello Laurie," she said with a quiver in her voice. "It has been tough here with Dad. He knows something is wrong because you wouldn't write the character reference, and you have not been in touch with him. He keeps asking me what's wrong and I've been putting him off. But today it just came out. I told him about you."

I could hardly breathe. "Really? What did you say?" How dare she do that without my permission! This was *my* story to tell.

"I told him that you had memories of being sexually abused and that's why you wouldn't write a letter in support of him after he was accused of fondling the boy in the swimming pool. It's also why you are not communicating with him. I know I should have waited until you were ready or at least until we discussed it, but it's too late for that."

I couldn't believe we were having this conversation. I could feel tingling in my fingers and toes as an electric current of shock poured through me.

"What did he say?" I asked.

"He vehemently denied it of course. He said your therapist was helping you generate false memories. I'm sorry," she said, her voiced laced with regret. "I shouldn't have said anything, but it just came out." She was asking for my forgiveness and understanding. I had none of that to give.

"Thanks for calling to tell me," I said.

"What are you going to do?"

I was furious. "I don't know yet, I need some time to think," I said. "Talk to you later."

Months earlier, I had a conversation with Dad at a deli in St. Louis where I told him that I believed he had touched me inappropriately, so it was not the first time he had heard the accusation. But to have someone else in the family talk to Dad and have no control over the narrative felt like a betrayal.

I had always been the well-behaved sister abiding by the rules. My maiden name was Goodman, and my childhood nickname was Goody. Now I had broken the cardinal rule by bringing up a family secret that had been buried and, my father hoped, forgotten. Maybe she wanted to take on the role of the good daughter and be understanding about Dad's frustration at being falsely accused. Was it possible that Shira defended me to Dad? Did she tell him that his behavior was unacceptable, even egregious?

The sting of betrayal of her telling Dad before I was ready and the pain of her getting angry at me aside, I wanted more. I wanted her to tell me she believed me. I wanted her to tell me what happened was not okay. I wanted her to thank me for doing the hard work of bringing the truth to the surface. I got none of that.

Dad didn't call me. I didn't call him either. I was not ready to talk. The following week he sent me a letter with the return address of the local chapter of the False Memory Syndrome Foundation. He said he was going to their meetings and suggested that I find one in my area. Their focus was confabulations created by inappropriate psychotherapy. I did not respond.

A week later Dad sent me a 25-page handwritten letter with 25 "good" memories listed. Memories, he said, are subjective. The exact same thing can happen to two people and they both perceive it differently. Reading the letter, nostalgia flooded my being.

- After choreographing special dances and gymnastics routines for Ben, Shira and me, Dad made up the names and countries we were from. He announced us from the back of the living room to an audience of family and friends.

- "Laurie LA-CAH-TOUR-EE-AY from France performing next!" he said, his hands cupped around his mouth like a carnival barker. I then ran full throttle to the front of the room and danced my heart out.

- Dad and Mom bought a small yellow trailer to travel in the summers. We went to the rolling hills of southern Illinois boating and swimming in Crab Orchard Lake during the day with Mom while Dad sold dry goods to the local discount stores with names like Grandpa Pigeon and Cousin Sue.

- He wrote an adaptation of a musical based off the songs in the movie *Chitty Chitty Bang Bang* called "*O City U City,*" (U City was an abbreviation for the suburb of St. Louis where we lived—University City). Ben and I along with other children in the neighborhood performed the musical and that helped spark my love for singing and dancing.

- He practiced with me for hours before my audition for my senior high school musical, *Sweet Charity.* When I got the lead role of Charity, he went over all my lines with me and coached me. When I didn't like the haircut I got just before opening night, he sat next to me and held my hand while I cried.

- He danced with me in our cavernous front hall with ten-foottall ceilings and a green and white checkered floor to elegant classical music coming from the record on the phonograph.

- He built me a rambling tree house in the backyard where I spent hours playing with the neighborhood children.

- He walked me down the aisle at my outdoor wedding in Lithia Park in the Sycamore Grove in Ashland, Oregon.

Dad was an excellent writer. He outlined each memory in detail, eloquently expressing his feelings about having that special time with me and emphasizing his deep love for me.

I was moved to tears after reading the letter. We did have some amazing memories together that were dear to my heart, but he was still denying the issue before us. These horrendously graphic memories coming into my consciousness after so many years were not minor events that could be dismissed as "being perceived differently."

There was no way my memories were false, and no False Memory Organization was going to convince me otherwise. It had been a long time since the sexual abuse happened, and Dad thought he was going to get off scot-free. But his vile acts were catching up with him at the end of his life. That young boy in the swimming pool and I were holding him accountable. In the dark recesses of his mind, he knew what he had done. He knew and he didn't want the truth to come out.

I wrote him back a few days later.

July 2003

Dear Dad,

I received your letter. It is unfortunate how this information came out. It is not my preference.

What happened is that when Shira called to ask me for a "letter of reference" for your lawyer, I refused to write it. I told her the reason why I couldn't write it was because I had been having memories resurface of childhood sexual and physical abuse from you. It was not my intention to talk to you about it because I knew you would deny it. I certainly have no desire to tell many people about it. It is something I prefer to keep as confidential as possible.

It is my understanding that you told your wife, Elle. That is your choice.

I have been through excruciating pain these last four months.

The memories have not come through "occult" or by "hypnosis" or "healing". They have come on their own—sometimes when I am alone, sometimes not. There have been many memories. When I remember, I have re-experienced the pain and it has been horrible. It has been difficult to function in my everyday life. I have been seeing a therapist for support.

I don't believe I am making these memories up. There are too many of them. They are too painful. They are too clear. I acknowledge that we have had many wonderful memories but those are not the ones that are wreaking havoc in my life.

I don't want to get into a discussion with you about whether I am making them up or not. No one would win such an argument. I am not going to change my belief that they happened. You are not going to change your belief that they didn't.

I am trying to find a way to cope, put this behind me and move on. It is hard to describe how painful it is and continues to be. I don't believe I would intentionally inflict this kind of pain on myself, and you, unless it was true.

I understand you have been diagnosed with a mental illness called "bipolar disorder." When a mental illness goes untreated, terrible things can happen. I believe that is what happened in my childhood. Mental illness is like any other illness; it needs to be treated and people who are mentally ill need help. That is my belief. I don't expect you to agree with me, but I think you need treatment. There are drugs and psychological treatments available.

Yes, there is a schism between us. What I experienced as a child was horrible beyond words. I understand that you are sick and need help and that still doesn't change the profound pain that I have experienced because of your actions and your untreated mental illness.

My focus right now is to do whatever I can to return to a normal life free of emotional and physical pain. This is my wish and everything I do is to help me achieve this goal.

Laurie

I don't know why I didn't mention Dad being arrested for fondling the boy in the swimming pool and being registered as a sexual offender. Those were facts that were on my side and could have bolstered my case. Ultimately, I don't think anything would have convinced Dad to admit what he did and tell the truth.

I was exhausted, rattled and outraged by the whole experience. How could he be getting away with this denial? It was so patently unfair. My fury dominated my every waking moment. A few days after I wrote the letter, I had a therapy session and went down into my subconscious through EMDR.

I saw Little Laurie around 7 years old, burned. My skin was on fire and then it turned black. I was in extreme pain, but no one would give me any treatment. I screamed at Mom and Dad telling them I needed to go to the burn center, but they kept reassuring me that everything was fine. I finally realized they weren't going to do anything. I wasn't dead. How was I going to survive this horrible pain?

My guides and angels came to help me. They told me they had to work quickly because otherwise I would be sent to a mental institution. I would be screaming and crying all the time and not able to do anything else, including going to school. They stuffed the charred skin away so I had normal looking skin on the outside, but it was still there.

After the session, an image came to me in a dream of the ships at Pearl Harbor the day the bombing happened, December 7, 1941. After doing some research, I found out most of the men were asleep on the ships when the bombs fell and could not escape. After the bombing was over, there were still several men left alive in the battleship *West Virginia*. The survivors could hear them pounding from the inside demanding to be rescued but the ship had taken on six torpedoes and two bombs, burned for 30 hours and settled in the mud at the bottom of the harbor. Cut a hole to get someone out and you've flooded the whole thing. Use a torch and you risk an explosion. They finally resolved they could not get them out alive.

No one wanted to do guard duty within earshot of the *West Virginia* because they didn't want to hear the desperate banging, the cries for help. Sixteen days passed and then silence.

Like the men in the battleship, my grief and anguish were calling to me as a 7-year-old child in muffled tones from underneath my skin, until I heard them no more. This was not something, as Dad suggested in his letter, I "perceived differently." This was a serious trauma.

The price I paid for hiding burnt skin and repressing the memories was the loss of a part of me. Unlike those men at Pearl Harbor who did not get a second chance, I now had the opportunity to retrieve that part of my soul that was lost when my angels and guides rescued me 40 years ago. I couldn't change Dad's perspective, but I could do my own healing. There was no going back. It was time to face the intense pain of third-degree burns and walk forward into the fire.

Marilyn

1978

Even after Bud resolved the property issue, I was ill at ease. The threat had not been withdrawn. I called the high school where our son was a junior, "We're taking Ben out of school for a few weeks to look at colleges. His life has been threatened."

In the meantime, Bud agreed to outfit our house with a burglar alarm. Such a task was not an easy prospect as we lived in a 14-room decaying mansion in University City, Missouri. I called our home Tara after Gone with the Wind. The home had a large wooden front porch with white columns reaching to the third-floor attic. The attic had a view of the entire city.

Then Bud reneged, "Sorry, it is too expensive. I've changed my mind," he said. "We can't install a burglar alarm."

I responded, "When it is our silver that is endangered, you make the decision. When it is our child, you have no choice." The burglar alarm was installed. The family called me the mother in charge of health and safety. That title would later haunt me.

I told Bud, "I can't stand what you're doing. If you don't drop this business, I'm leaving you."

He said "You're right. I'm dropping this messy business."

I soon discovered that he had no intention of quitting, but such was my state that I did not move out immediately. I had not left Bud seven years earlier when the gonorrhea traveled up my coil and infected my fallopian tubes. At the time, Bud was furious that I had enrolled in a doctoral program in education at the University of Missouri in St. Louis. All he could articulate, however, was "What in the world can you ever do with a doctorate in Community Education?"

I was in such pain that I needed to do yoga exercises in the morning and evening. I sought alternative doctors. My digestive organs never totally healed.

Only the winter after our son's life was threatened and Bud insisted on keeping the thermostat at 56 degrees to cut down on the $700 a month heating bill, did I finally get the gumption to walk out and move to my mother's apartment. Albeit it was just a few months after I discovered he was still acting as a "pimp". I had asked mother for the key before she left for Clearwater Beach, Florida. Oddly **cold** *was the straw that broke the camel's back.*

Chapter Eighteen

Thirtieth High School Reunion July 2003

The four of us sat in a small booth with torn seats in the back corner of a greasy spoon restaurant: Dad, his wife Elle, my cousin Alice and me. Alice was a single woman a decade older than me. We were never close, but she'd always been kind to me and knew Dad well, which made her the perfect buffer and ally.

"I'm flying back to St. Louis for my high school reunion," I told her when I'd called her a week before. "Would you like to join Dad, Elle and me for lunch?"

"Sure," she said, delighted to be included. I didn't reach out to her often. Nothing was said about the sexual abuse allegations or the letters. To this day I don't know if she was aware of Dad's recent arrest and conviction for sexual molestation.

I picked Alice up and we drove to the restaurant. If she noticed that I was nervous, she didn't say anything. When Dad and Elle walked into the restaurant, my heart was pounding out of my chest. We hugged each other and sat down. I filled Dad in on the latest news of the family carrying the conversation with very little input from any of them.

While I was with him, I looked into his eyes and told myself that this is the man in my memories. He is guilty. I didn't make this up. It was still hard to connect the painful memories with this man I loved so much, but I did not doubt myself anymore. We did not discuss the letters or any of our feelings.

The book, *Leaving the Saints,* was my bible in 2003 and Martha Beck, the author, my heroine. Martha said it was so difficult to write but it really helped her with her pain. The first chapter opens with a confrontation with her father where Martha alleges that he sexually abused her, and he denies it. She faces him head on with strength and conviction, her story not to be denied.

I wanted to be the heroine in my story as well. I have relived that lunch with Dad repeatedly in my head in the years since wishing I'd said something when I had the chance. But the truth is, I was not ready at that time in my life to confront him knowing he would deny my allegations. I just did not have the emotional bandwidth. Little Laurie was not ready either. She told me she didn't feel safe confronting him in person. I finally understand that even though the big declaration scene didn't happen, it makes my story no less valid.

We went on a walk after lunch, and I took advantage of a moment alone with Dad to give him a message.

"I need some time and space," I told him. He did not respond. I told Alice I was ready to leave, hugged Dad and Elle, and walked off not knowing when or if I would ever see him again.

The next day, I went to see Mom. Her apartment was small and neat with a place for pieces of furniture from our childhood including the simple wooden rocking chair where she had nursed us as children which she had refinished with a new gorgeous, embroidered seat. There were large windows that looked out over a grove of oak trees.

She fixed me a delicious breakfast. We sat at the small table next to an elaborate brown hutch that looked too big and imposing in the small space. The fold-out plain brown table was set with sterling silverware and the pale green china she received as a wedding present. I brought up our phone conversation about the abuse memories as soon as we sat down.

"I believe you," she said immediately. "It puts a lot of the pieces of the puzzle together. Now I understand why they put you in the slow class in first-grade. You were so spacy. You wet the bed until you were 8 or 9 years old." Her head was down, and she talked softly. I could feel the anger rising in me as she spoke.

"Yes. Several of the terrifying events happened in the bathroom," I told her. "I still have bladder issues."

"I am shocked and ashamed that I didn't know. Especially now that we know about what happened in the swimming pool, it is clear he has a serious problem." Her eyes pleaded with me to understand.

"I believe you," I said.

As we sat around her rickety table, I felt a sense of relief and gratitude that she believed the abuse happened. But I also felt intense anger. The anger was so volatile, it was hard to keep my composure. I'm sure she felt my anger, but she said nothing.

"Do you wish I hadn't married your Dad and you had never been born?" she asked. I snapped my head around in surprise.

"No, of course not," I said. "I love my life. I want to be here." What kind of a question was that? Was she trying to look on the bright side by saying at least I was born? I didn't want to get in an argument, so I let it go.

Mom and I parted awkwardly. I told her I would keep in touch. I kept our time together brief because my emotions were so volatile. I said I believed her that she did not know about the sexual abuse at the time but a part of me did not believe her. How could she put it together so easily now and not know what was happening then? She must have had an inkling something was amiss and just didn't have the guts to admit it.

The next day, I got up early and went on a tour of my high school with my fellow 1973 graduates. University City High School was built in 1930 in the Art Deco style. Its deep sense of history enveloped me when I entered. There was a presence and pride to the building that was substantial and so unlike the flimsy prefab schools where I worked for many years in California.

There were about 30 of us on the tour being led by a student from the leadership class. We walked up the wide stairs through the main doors and went in. I saw my playbill as star of the senior musical *Sweet Charity* in 1973 in a glass case in the entryway. My eyes welled up remembering the joy I experienced in playing the role of Charity.

Most of us on the tour had been in music class together, so when we arrived on the third floor and walked into the music room, we were transported back in time as we found our seats. The men sat in the tenor and bass section, the women in the alto and soprano. We all spontaneously began to sing the chorus from *Swing Low Sweet Chariot.* Chills went up my arms as I remembered my joy singing with these young men and women.

In my high school days, I was eager to walk the mile and a half to school to start early school chorus at 6:30 am with my best friend Leslie. Singing while I looked from my spot in the alto section through the floor to ceiling windows out over the treetops was the highlight of my morning. The music teacher Mr. T had a way of making me feel like he truly cared not just about my singing but about me as a person. I felt totally seen by him. Mom told me for many years she would bump into Mr. T while doing errands and he always asked about me and how I was doing. I never went back to see Mr. T after I left high school to let him know how special he was to me. When I read his obituary several years ago, I deeply regretted that oversight.

When the tour was over, I walked the three blocks down to the Jackson Street house where I had lived until I was in fourth grade. Dark green ivy crawled up the red brick and the green shutters were now painted a dark red. The house looked small, unassuming and innocent. On the north side, I saw my upstairs bedroom window where I spent many nights talking to the moon.

No one was home, so I snuck into the backyard and saw the sloping grass that went into a stand of oak trees. I remembered a recent memory that had come through where I was about 6 years old and saw myself playing in those trees and then Dad came out, wrestling me to the ground and laid on top of me. I looked at the backyard and brought the memory into my consciousness. It felt important to ground myself, to make it real, this small house and shady, peaceful place where so many traumatic events had occurred. It *really did happen* and I survived. I have even thrived. I was proud of that fact.

Marilyn

2003

Apparently, it was at this time that our daughter Laurie's suppressed memories began to resurface. Laurie had planned a visit, alone, to St. Louis for a few days before she attended an interpreting conference in Chicago to visit one of her former classmates who had cancer. She did not change her plans.

Bud had written Laurie a nasty letter denying any wrongdoing, but Laurie still wanted to visit and did go out to dinner with her father and his wife and cousin. Laurie said they did not talk about anything personal. Bud never said he was sorry or ever admitted making a mistake.

My visit with Laurie was over breakfast. I prepared my famous fresh grapefruit, orange juice drink with yogurt and strawberries whipped in a blender. I served an omelet with red peppers, mushrooms and green peppers arranged on my best china.

Afterwards, we walked to the JCC pool to swim. Sounds idyllic, but it was hard. I said again I was sorry, and Laurie told more of her story.

At six, she said, "I was back on the screened porch at 1077 Jackson. You remember the porch Mom, don't you? I wanted to die. I was so squashed with pain and fear from Dad's sexual assaults. Then angels appeared. They slid down on moonbeams and told me that I must live. They would support me. I had work to do in this life. I told Dad he could never touch me again. Once I saw him look askance at Shira (our middle daughter). I told him if he ever touched her, I would kill him."

Apparently, her Dad took her seriously because he did not abuse Shira or touch Laurie again. Bud had always complained to me that I was too lenient with the children. They were good kids; I didn't see what the problem was. I never would have thought he was "disciplining" Laurie by telling her she was so bad he must punish her with a sexual assault.

Chapter Nineteen

Time to Heal

When I came home from my high school reunion, the memories stopped. All the adrenaline and energy I used to deal with trauma had drained away and I was more exhausted than I had been in my life. I had the summer off from work and spent most of my time in bed staring at the wall. Whatever had kept me going before was no longer there.

Mom called a few weeks after I got back.

"I'm really upset about everything you shared with me," she said.

"It is *very* upsetting. I am grateful that you believe me. I don't understand why you didn't notice something was wrong! I was wetting the bed until I was 9 years old and not doing well in school."

"I know." she said. "Looking back, I feel so stupid that I didn't pick up on it." She started crying. "I'm so sorry," she sobbed. I waited a little while for her sobs to calm down.

"Mom, I can't be your emotional support through this," I said,

"Let's talk about something else."

"I'm still writing of course," she said. "But now I am writing about your revelations."

"I'm not ready to hear your writing," I said. We were both quiet as we searched for something to talk about

"Why don't I call you back next week when we both have had time to cool off?" I suggested.

"Ok." she said reluctantly.

In Novermber 2003, I got a terrible bladder infection. When my body-worker, Ken, asked me to close my eyes and focus on the bladder, an image came into my mind's eye of a glacier resting on my bladder. As I communicated with the glacier, it told me it represented my anger at my parents and my sister.

A few days later in therapy with Paul, I closed my eyes and focused on the glacier. The following image came up for me.

> *I was about 7 years old. Mom and Dad were fighting, and I was watching them with huge eyes, terrified. Mom left and Dad came towards me, furious. He was yelling, and when I didn't respond, he started choking me. I was gasping for air thinking I'd die but he finally let go of me. When I recovered, I ran into the kitchen and grabbed a knife from the cutting block. I whirled around to face him, and he twisted the knife out of my hand. I leaned over and threw up.*

After the session, I was so exhausted I could barely move. I sat on my bed the next day, closed my eyes, and had a conversation with my guardian angel, Mariah. She told me I needed to take space from my primary family for a while. It was important for my healing process. I took some time to discuss it with my therapist and decided to let my family know I would not be communicating with them until I felt ready to do so.

There was no need to call Dad as I had made it clear to him in our last meeting that I needed time to heal, and I didn't know if or when we would talk again. I called my brother Ben and gave him a perfunctory explanation. He was confused and I think a bit overwhelmed and surprised, but kind and accepting. Mom was devastated. She started crying and could not stop. I felt sad and guilty, but I was determined to take care of myself. The hardest one to call was Shira. I knew I had to do it, but I was shaking with fear and dread. Dealing with her at all at this point was more than I could bear.

"I need to take some time away from the family in order to heal," I said.

"I understand," she said. "Take whatever time you need." Her voice was kind and understanding.

"Thank you," I said.

When we discussed this conversation after I had reconnected with Shira, she said that I told her I might never want to talk to her again. I sincerely don't remember saying that, but it was entirely possible. At that point, I needed relief like I needed air and talking to family was not something I could even fathom.

I hadn't felt any support for spilling the family secrets except from my brother who really wasn't involved. Mom, Dad and Shira had only added to my pain. Dad was in denial. Shira was blaming me for telling her too much and asked me not to discuss it anymore and Mom was asking me to take care of her. I needed time to deal with my own feelings about the memories bubbling up into consciousness without any interaction with them. It was a relief. Of course, I had Michael and the children to deal with, but that felt manageable.

I didn't know or care how long I would need before I talked to my family again. I would take as long as necessary for what felt like an essential component of my survival. Anger and fear were pulling me under into dark, rough quicksand and I was waving the white flag of surrender just before I disappeared. I needed time to process and let the overwhelming pain engulf me.

Marilyn

2003

Laurie continued, "I am working on forgiving both you and Dad. I am not there yet. I need space. After I go home, I think it is best not to talk for a while. I've told Dad the same thing. Of course, you can still keep in touch with the children. I do hope you understand, mother. I'm taking art therapy, seeing a psychologist, and taking cranial therapy treatments."

Later Laurie decided to cut off communication with her siblings as well. Laurie, the strong backbone of the family, was pulling away to heal herself. On paper, I gave her encouragement. I wrote to her the best way she could support me was to take care of herself. Still the pain seems fresh, but it is beginning to heal in these last nine months in which Laurie and I have talked just in passing and only once or twice when she happens to answer the phone. She did send me a card on my birthday saying she hoped I understood why she needed space.

December 2004
From Mom's journal:

Right now the pain of thinking I never will see my offspring and their offspring again brings a grief so unimaginable that I can hardly breathe. But only the wind can hear my tears. Surely that will not come to pass. I should be blessed for telling the truth, for believing Laurie, for asking how I could support her. I am blessed for admitting my mistakes.

Chapter Twenty

Five Years

Mom (on the right) with her friend of over 50 years, 2011

When I went to therapy in December of 2003, I journeyed down into my subconscious through EMDR and received a vision of a crystal ball. Inside the ball, I saw Mom just like Dorothy saw her Aunty Em. Mom's eyes were filled with pain as she stared out into space. I couldn't handle the knot that welled up in my stomach so I asked the ball to go black.

Responsible. I could feel that word echoing in my psyche. *My fault. Her pain is my fault.* My heart hurt.

My therapist Paul looked at me piercingly and said, "Sometimes as children we feel that if we are responsible then it gives us some control. But it doesn't work when we become adults and it is still embedded in our psyche."

"But I *am* responsible." I said. "I am the one who cut off communication with her."

"You are not responsible for her feelings," Paul said. "You are not responsible for *her.*"

But I felt responsible, nonetheless. The guilt was like a constant gnawing in my gut. I asked myself often if this was the right decision. But I did not call her.

I recently watched the documentary *Finding Neverland* about two boys who Michael Jackson sexually abused. One of the boys was James Safechuck. James explained over the four hour documentary how he was raped by Michael Jackson for years. The consequences of that reverberated into his adult life and devastated everything in its path. In the final scene of the movie, James was asked if he had forgiven his mother, Stephanie. He hesitated and after a long pause said he was working on it.

Stephanie, in her interview, when asked how she felt about taking Michael's word for it when he said he was only sleeping in the same bed with her son but not having sex, said she didn't protect her son, and it would always haunt her. She had one job and she messed up.

Mom didn't protect me. Mom, who declared herself "the person in charge of health and safety", who didn't allow me to slide down the banister backwards so I wouldn't fall off, who made me hold her hand while we were crossing the street so I wouldn't get hit by a car, who wouldn't let me swim until an hour after I ate so I wouldn't get stomach cramps, was nowhere to be found when my father molested me.

Shira and I argued recently about how many years I cut off my primary family. She said it was five years and I said it was two years. I looked it up in my journal and Shira was right. It didn't feel like five years at the time. It felt more like five minutes. Time has a funny way of being skewed by pain. Five years. No family holidays. No phone conversations. No contact. No seeing the grandchildren. No time together as cousins. Silence.

What did I do for those five years? In my mid-40s, I was busy working during the day and taking care of the kids at night. I wasn't thinking about Mom's reality of being retired and wondering how long it would be until she could see me and my family again. Would it be before she passed away?

Now that I am closer to the age Mom was then and retired myself, I have such empathy for her. Five years is a long time. But at the time, for me, it was survival. I needed to be able to live my life and work through the pain in therapy, in my journaling, in screaming out to the universe, in any way I could without the interruption of dealing with my primary family.

It was the beginning of 2008 when I finally was ready to reach out to my family again. I made the decision in therapy. The reconnection was choppy and messy with many hurt feelings all around.

I tried to connect with Ben in person at a restaurant in San Francisco but had to leave because he reminded me too much of Dad with his voice and facial expressions. I told him I was sorry, it was not his fault and ran out.

Shira was mad that I hadn't talked to her in so long and it was hard to connect on a deeper level with that elephant in the room between us. We had therapy on the phone to deal with her pain about the silent years. But we didn't deal with *my* pain because that subject was off limits.

Mom wanted to come to visit me so we could talk in person. I was not ready to have her come to my house, so I booked a hotel room for us. I was shocked to see how much older she looked. At 77 years old, she was bent over and moved carefully with great strain. I felt a wrenching sadness when I thought about the years I missed with her and knew she would not have many more.

We went to out to eat at a restaurant called *The Slanted Door* in San Francisco. Sitting at the table looking at the beauty of the San Francisco Bay at sunset, I fidgeted with the napkin in my lap. It was hard to pick a safe topic. I knew mentioning my kids would bring Mom fresh pain. Although I didn't prevent my children from talking with Mom, communication was very infrequent. They knew I had cut off communication with my primary family and it affected their relationships with their grandparents, aunts, uncles and cousins. I regret that I did not share the truth with Noah and Rachel. I left it vague. I told myself I was trying to protect them. But I was only perpetuating the big lie.

"I've started a new business called *Elders Probe the Arts*," Mom said. "We pair older people with younger people, and they mentor them on various art forms including poetry and writing."

"How is that going?" I asked.

"It is wonderful," she gushed. "Everyone is getting so much out of it." As she talked about her new business, my eyes glazed over.

"Sounds like an excellent idea," I said half-heartedly. I did appreciate Mom's talent and creativity, but I was having a hard time staying present. I felt like I was jumping high on a trampoline, my stomach in my throat, not sure what the next bounce would bring.

After dinner, we went to a movie called *The Diving Bell and the Butterfly* about a man locked inside his body with no way to communicate except blinking his eyes. We both were fascinated by the movie and were relieved to have something to talk about. It was too much seeing Mom again and not enough. I was ready to go back home the next morning, but Mom cajoled me into taking a short time to write poetry together in our hotel room.

Someone Calls a Child's Name

BY MARILYN PROBE

January 26, 2008

While all the others are away, as we without words re-tread,
my daughter and I forgo our tears,
hiding the trauma behind our veneers.

Like bark that grows over shards in the arms of the tree, we shed
our past, skirting the tissue of truth, until a movie unwinds the tears
locked in the bell of our minds.
She echoes words my son has spoken.

"It's a visceral thing, not speaking to the brother I love. It's a reach
for me to finish healing." Sorrow opens our hearts that were broken.
We meld with each other,
our first visit in years, softening our breach.

Our dreams lean toward each other, understanding our quest,
the pulse of our flesh, as I reflect and configure
an infant's touch, the diminutive lips on the breast.

The daughter commences to nourish the mother,
an opening bar in a fugue of forgiveness, as fingers
pirouette a silent language--before, after, under.

Watching My Mother Put On Her Two Coats

BY LAURIE JACOBVITZ

January 26, 2008

She reads me poetry.
I cannot write poems
Don't listen to that voice.
Sun streams in the room as we write

35 years ago singing "Hallelujah Chorus" in the morning
I cry
Music, I miss music.
Singing. Yes. Sing more.
Life is short.

Watching my mother take out her hearing aid
Giving her ears a rest

She sighs
Cherish the gift of hearing.

Pine caskets
Embalming
Burial
I hear the words.
Breathe in the pain.

Breathe out impatience
Breathe in joy
Breathe out anger
Breathe in forgiveness
Breathe out harshness
Breathe in love.

Watching my mother write
Her hand glides across the page
Her creativity strong, alive.
Beautiful words.

Watching my mother put on her coats
I am impatient
Wanting to move quickly
Breathe. Stay in the present.
Bright fuchsia, pale blue, full paisley scarf with tassels

She cannot live forever.
Her love is with me always.

SILENCE

BY MARILYN PROBE

December 2005

Silence now broken by the drill of a woodpecker, whippoorwill and repetitive tone of an invisible bird.

Silence of a child in outer space when violated

Silence of lips before they touch forbidden spaces

Silence broken, memories resurfacing after 40 years.

Silence of fields sprayed with insecticide.

Poison of not knowing, festering wounds that did not heal

Cardinals, wrens, sparrows silenced by cicadas clacking wings.

Fireflies dancing at twilight, send flames over a meadow

Silent like the big dipper and the moon, so still it's invisible tonight

Sky painted sienna strokes of smoke
Like the screen you didn't know was there, the barrier of four decades

That has finally been permeated like the sudden squawk of the
great blue heron, his yellow beak flashing, body streamline
like a missile diving into air
Punctuating silence like the sound of your daughter's voice on
a summer morning screaming
"You think Adolphus was abused, what about me?"

Chapter Twenty-One

Chapter 21 Dad's Final Year

Even though I was ready to reach out to the others in my family in 2008, I still was not ready to contact Dad in person. Little Laurie begged me not to see him, so I complied. I did, however, respond to his letters.

September 14, 2008

Dear Dad,

I have adapted to the computer age. It is easier for me to type my letter and make edits as I go along. I want to thank you for the time you took to write your heartfelt letter. I appreciate your willingness to communicate.

I will do my best to respond to all your comments and questions and if I miss anything, please let me know. To begin with, as far as my lack of communication these last five years, there was a part of me that really wanted to contact you and share what I was going through (it was a constant inner battle), but I was too scared. I just couldn't do it, until now.

About eight years ago, I started having chronic vaginal yeast infections. Nothing would cure them. Then about five years ago, I went into a deep depression for no reason that I could see. I didn't want to eat and I couldn't sleep. I was exhausted all the time. I decided to go to therapy. I got in touch with my feelings and that is when the memories started coming up. Please understand that I did not do hypnosis in therapy. My therapist did not mention or suggest at any time that you may have molested me as a child. He just helped me get in touch with my feelings and the memories of sexual abuse spontaneously started coming up. They would come up mostly outside of therapy—in the bathtub, when I woke up in the morning, when I was taking a walk. The memories were varied and there were many of them. They were very painful to remember emotionally. It was difficult to lead my life and deal with them. It was very painful physically as well. I do not believe that I would make them up for no reason. That makes no sense.

I was not aware of any "epidemic" in California of people having false memory syndrome (FMS). I did not talk to other people in California about my memories (other than my therapist) or go to any support groups, nor did I have any desire to. It was a completely personal experience. When you sent me the letters about false memory syndrome, I talked to my therapist about it and he told me that FMS is a valid phenomenon. But, it is not what I experienced. I had repressed memories--which are also a valid phenomenon—that came to the surface on their own without any suggestion or fabrication. The memories all happened between the ages of approximately 4 to 7 years old and the majority of them happened in the Jackson Street house. As far as any other details, I do not feel comfortable sharing them with you.

To clear up the issue with the phone call with Shira, Shira actually called me to ask me to write an affidavit, a character reference for you, because your lawyer had requested it for a trial that was going on. I could not do that in good conscience because the memories had just started surfacing at that time. I told her I would call her back. I really was not ready to talk to anyone in the family about the memories. But, I felt I had to give her some reason and the truth was the best idea. When I called her back, the purpose of the conversation was to explain to her why I could not do the character reference. I told her that I believed you had sexually abused me as a child. That was it. I did not try to convince her that she was sexually abused. That is not for me to say. Other than clearing up that one issue, which I hope I have done, I would prefer to keep Shira and Ben out of this. I would prefer to keep this between us only.

That all being said, the reason I contacted you again is not to convince you that these memories actually happened. That is not my intent. Conversely, you are not going to convince me that what happened to me was false memory syndrome. I got in touch with you in the hope and with the intent that we could have some peace and ease in our current relationship.

I understand that you feel very strongly that you have been accused of something you did not do and that it has caused you a great deal of pain and anguish. I believe it happened. I don't understand why you did it. I don't understand why the memories surfaced when they did. There are many things in life that maybe I will never understand but this I know...Human beings are all connected and we are all one. I cannot separate myself from you no matter how hard I try. Looking back, I don't know if my five years of silence with you on this issue was right or not. But, those years are gone and we can only go forward from here.

I love you Dad

Laurie

September 23, 2008

Dear Dad,

I understand that you consider yourself an innocent victim in all of this.

You are very angry and blame me for people in the family dis-

tancing themselves from you. You believe I am making unfair accusations with no proof to back it up. Your reputation has been damaged and it is my fault.

Let me remind you that I am not the only one who has accused you. You have been found guilty in a court of law and your picture is on the internet as a sexual offender.

You want to have a conversation with me where I go through each memory you have shared one by one and explain how you remember it differently. In that way you will prove that the memories were untrue. You also want more details about my memories of abuse so you can refute them.

I understand your requests. I am just not willing to honor them. I have already said that I do not feel comfortable sharing any more information about the memories. I stand by that statement.

Laurie

When I said in my letter I was "wanting some peace and ease in our current relationship," with this huge elephant in the room between us, that was unrealistic. I saw Dad a couple of times during family gatherings that last year before he died and even though we didn't interact, I regret attending family events and pretending like everything was fine again. I was condoning sweeping the family secrets under the rug and setting the tone for years to come.

Dad was diagnosed with dementia towards the end of my five years of no communication. Do I think dementia affected his memory of the abuse? No. He denied abusing me in 2003 just after he touched the boy's genitals in the swimming pool. Like most men accused of sexual assault, Dad went with the "didn't happen" argument.

In early 2009, Shira called to say that he would wander away from the house without his wife knowing. One time, they could not find him for hours, so we all decided he needed to be put in a nursing home. I flew back to St. Louis to do research and visit potential places.

Dad was on Medicaid and could not afford assisted living or the pricier facilities for people with memory loss. The smell of urine and feces as I toured the nursing homes are still seared into my memory. In one location, I was aghast to see at least 50 people wandering around a room drooling and mumbling to themselves. I ran out the door. My brother and I hired a lawyer at $500 an hour but we found she really didn't have much more to offer than what we could find on our own.

We finally found a decent placement after what seemed like endless research, but they rejected him at the last minute because they found out he was a registered sex offender. I was so angry! Now people were finally setting limits for him when he could barely get out of bed! We ended up going with a place that was not our first choice, but it was clean and decent and would have to do.

I visited him there once in August of 2009 when I was traveling across the country with my son Noah. We drove in a moving truck together to North Carolina where Noah would be starting his PhD program at Duke University.

Dad was lying on a narrow bed in the corner with a vacant look in his eyes. Noah hung back not knowing what to say.

"Hi Dad," I said.

There was no response.

"Noah and I are driving across the country, and we thought we would stop by and say hello." There was still no movement to acknowledge our presence. I sat down on the bed and he jerked away from me. The energy emanating from him was dark and angry. I was really shaken up and we left a few minutes later. That was the last time I saw him.

My husband and children now knew about the abuse and didn't want to attend the funeral when Dad passed in November of 2009, so I flew back to St. Louis alone. There were 30 or 40 people there, mostly family.

The night after the funeral, I dreamed I was at Dad's house on Cabanne Avenue in St. Louis. Dad was sitting in a room full of people in a rocking chair.

"Look there's Dad!" I said with surprise. "I thought he was dead." Then he slowly faded into the background and was gone. I didn't feel any grief with Dad's passing. I kept waiting for the grief to hit me, but it never did.

About a year after he died, when I was visiting friends and family in St. Louis, I decided to drive to Jefferson Barracks, the military cemetery where he was buried. After checking the map and getting lost, I finally found the right section, but there were hundreds of small white tombstones all the same size and I had no idea how long it would take to find his grave. I soon realized that most people were Christian and had a cross on their tombstone. As I walked down the aisles, I looked for the Jewish Star of David and finally saw the stone with Dad's name on it—Bernard B. Goodman. I stood there for a while in silence. Then I took a white handkerchief out of my pocket and slowly waved it giving Dad the white handkerchief treatment, the family tradition. The handkerchief fluttered in the wind like the white flag of surrender.

"Goodbye Dad," I said and walked away for good.

Marilyn

2003

What did I learn? There are no absolute truths. That I was cast in this drama in the same shoes as my ex, the children's father. With the family split apart, I need to develop a new life.

During the previous year, before Laurie's repressed memories surfaced, Shira invited me to bring over and share dinner with her and my grand-children every other Thursday. We had a better relationship than we ever had before. That was to change. Shira, my middle daughter, with whom I had so happily worked with on Earth Day the previous year, would soon want more space to herself, giving her time to heal. She felt betrayed by her father. She wrote to Laurie, "Do not communicate with me. I didn't read all of your email. I don't want to know all the details of what Dad did to you."

I would learn what I always knew, to forgive myself, I would need to totally forgive my ex. I certainly had more empathy for him than I had. We were cast in the same shadow as perpetrators. I am writing more and talking less. I fixed up the country cottage with a wood stove to extend the season there. I added a phone for communication and emergencies. I will visit more often, plant more hyacinths, daisies, collards, basil, sage, red and white onions; dig deep in the earth.

I will continue to pray to the moon for my children. Although they now want breathing space, there is still hope as Laurie says that they will heal, and we will come together again. I will be here if they need me. I now feel divorced from my girls or an orphan in reverse. I will take good care of myself and be open to the love that I meet each day.

Epilogue

It is possible to live a happy and fulfilling life after a traumatic childhood. I do have such a life and am grateful for it every day. I hope this book will give others belief that they or those they love who have been through something similar can do the same.

I discovered Mom's memoir *Fractured, I Grow Stronger* after I finished the first draft of my memoir. Before reading it, I had never heard about the family secrets of Dad giving Mom sexually transmitted diseases or acting as a pimp. I was shocked but it also validated my perspective that Dad's behavior was seriously out of control. I didn't realize that Mom was doing her own reflecting on the past. After the disclosure of my memories, the pool incident and seeing the movie *Capturing the Friedman's,* she accepted the fact that sexual abuse did happen in her home.

I decided to include the main excerpts from her memoir to corroborate my truth from a different perspective. I also wanted to include her poetry because she is such an accomplished poet and it was her dying wish to have more of her poems published. Mom believed me when I told her that Dad physically and sexually assaulted me. For that, I am eternally grateful. I was still angry at her, however, for not protecting me. In 2008, we decided to go to therapy with her therapist. I thought her therapist was lousy, but I was willing to give it some time. After a few sessions, Mom said, "I don't want to talk about the past anymore." And that was it. We stopped therapy and did not discuss Dad's molestation again.

Dad stayed in denial until the day he died in November of 2009. He never accepted the truth. I say the truth because I know beyond a shadow of a doubt that my father physically and sexually abused me as a child. Dad skated by with only a few weekends in jail because one boy was willing to press charges when Dad fondled him in the swimming pool. Who knows how many other nameless people were harmed and no one else said anything, until now, until after his death, when I had the courage to do so.

After Dad was diagnosed with bipolar disorder at the age of 80 years old, I went online and found an article called "*The Connection Between Bipolar Disorder and Hypersexuality*" by Marcia Purse on *verywellmind.com* (July 27, 2022). Marcia discussed the connection between bipolar disorder and hypersexuality as a symptom of the upcycle of bipolar or mania. She mentioned that sometimes during a manic episode, sex can become compulsive and addictive which leads to such behaviors as having multiple affairs outside of marriage and sexually abusing children. I stared at the words for a long time taking them in. The article recommended finding the right mix of medications to prevent hypersexuality from becoming destructive. My father refused to take medications. He refused to admit he was mentally ill at all.

"Such behaviors such as sexually abusing children," it said. There it was in black and white. Those words seemed so benign printed on the page, but they changed my life forever. Mom getting sexually transmitted diseases also fit with the description of Dad's mental illness and the resulting sexual addiction. Untreated mentally ill people have been a nightmare for many families, including mine.

Dad was ill and ultimately lost control over his behavior. That doesn't condone what he did to me and countless others. Learning about the Epstein Files, it is shocking to me how many legions of men, like my father, are wreaking havoc on young girls' lives. I am furious that these men have gotten away with pedophilia and sexual abuse for so long and continue to do so. I want to do what I can to help which includes publishing this book and coming out of the closet as an incest survivor.

Forgiving Dad is not a split-second process. Anger and forgiveness can co-exist. But I am committed to the ongoing work of bringing more peace and ease into my life while honoring my feelings.

I also forgive myself for not having "the conversation" with Dad where I confront him about what he did. For not speaking to my primary family for five years. For sweeping things under the rug after I knew about the abuse and still going to family events with Dad and pretending like everything was fine. For not believing in Little Laurie for so long. For perpetuating and keeping the family secrets. For not telling my children the truth about why we weren't seeing my family. For not having more empathy for my sister and what she was going through. There are so many things I wish I had done differently. Berating myself won't help. Loving and forgiving myself is crucial.

And, of course, I forgive Mom. It was so difficult for me to read about her pain and to know that I missed five years with her at the end of her life. I wish I could have forgiven her earlier, but I was not ready.

After I read her memoir, I had so many questions for Mom. Why didn't she tell me her secrets while she was alive? Why didn't she leave Dad? Would she be all right with me including excerpts of her memoir in my memoir?

I wanted to find a way to communicate with her directly, so I decided to have a session with my spiritual therapist, Kat, and we invited Mom's spirit to be with us. Kat had me visualize a safe space to meet with Mom and we called in my guides and my guardian angel, Mariah. I saw myself in a hammock that looked like a cocoon. It was made of soft gauzy white material and surrounded me completely. I sunk into it and it felt like a soft cloud. The room was filled with the light of love.

When Kat called Mom's spirit in, Mom was sobbing so hard that snot was coming out of her nose. She kept saying, "I'm sorry" repeatedly. That was Mom. She was definitely a crier. I asked her to calm down and told her I had some questions for her. She dried her eyes and looked at me with such deep love. One thing I never doubted was that Mom loved me. She would send me cards on Valentine's Day, special watercolor handmade cards, and tell me why she loved me so much. One time she gave me $300 for no reason whatsoever and told me to treat myself.

"Go to a spa or some out of the way secluded spot," she said. "I just want you to be happy. I don't care what you are doing in your life. If you are happy, that makes me happy." She was constantly sending me love and blessings.

"How do you feel about me including your memoir in my memoir?" I asked.

I received a holographic download from her filled with impressions, feelings and images without words. I could feel Mom's love, pride and confidence in me. I was relieved to know she did not have any limits on what I could share. I did not feel any concern from her about publishing my memoir. That was a huge relief to me. "You are an excellent writer." I told her. I could see her relax and smile at my compliment.

"Why didn't you tell me about Dad being a pimp, you getting physically scarred from STDs and the depth of the trauma you endured in your marriage?"

The energy I felt was that this was the perfect time for me to find out that information. I would not have been able to receive it in the same way before now.

"Why did you wait so long to leave Dad?"

I saw Mom floating above her body in a cloud with only a slender rope tethering her. She was suspended there unable to fully enter her body. There were only pieces of her fully incarnated and those pieces were a hodgepodge of discombobulated images. My heart bled for her and one word came to mind--dissociation.

The University of Washington published an article called "*What is Dissociation and What to Do About It?*" (July 2022). They describe dissociation as an escape valve in response to trauma in your life. When physical escape is not possible, then you can escape mentally by pretending that the trauma is not happening. Some typical behaviors are spacing out or daydreaming as well as detachment from the self or identity.

This describes Mom perfectly as she was often emotionally unavailable and partially present. I would ask her questions, and she would take a long time to respond or not respond at all. She was often in a different world.

Mom then showed me a feeling of being inexorably pulled to Dad. There was an intense attraction, like a moth to a flame. The energy felt dark like a black viscous liquid that surrounded the two of them and glued her to his side. I could feel how hard it was to extricate herself from that. It was easier to give in than try and fight it. The energy Dad emitted was both alluring, repulsive and sticky. Seeing those images and feeling them kinesthetically helped me understand her actions.

"Do you think Dad was mentally ill?" I asked.

Mom sent me a feeling of rightness like puzzle pieces clicking into place. She showed me how the seeds of mental illness within Dad were spurred on to blossom by the trauma of World War II followed by the emotional devastation of his brother's death. I felt overwhelming love from her and the guides and angels surrounding us. I was filled with gratitude and peace.

Acknowledgements

To my husband Michael Jacobvitz, you have been there for me every step of the way from my first traumatic memories to writing this book. Your love has lifted me up and been a huge part of my healing process. Thank you for the long insightful conversations that I cherish. I am indeed blessed to have you in my life. I love you.

To my friend Danny Miller, you were there supporting me and encouraging me throughout the whole writing process. You also had the idea of integrating Mom's memoir with mine by putting an excerpt of her memoir that related to what I had written in between each chapter in a braided style. That transformed this book.

To my friend Grace Manning, you give so generously of your time and surround me with your love. When I talk with you, I feel rejuvenated. You have seen me through so much of the healing process. Thank you so much for being a beta reader and giving me honest feedback and for the years of free tarot readings.

To my friend, Heidi Brockmann, thank you for all your support, for taking laughing classes together, doing yoga together, listening to me with a full and open heart and for being a beta reader.

To my friend and fellow writer, Jane Tomiasson, thank you for all your support and love.

To my friend Gina Batti you believed in me when I didn't believe in myself and told me this book has an energy of its own and wants to be published. Thank you for being my writing buddy.

To Becky Turner, my friend from childhood, thank you for having a safe house I could go to across the street and for keeping in touch all these years. Thank you for being a beta reader and loving and supporting me.

To my friend Donna Clendennin, thank you for being a beta reader and giving me honest feedback.

To my memoir class teacher, Dani Burlison, thank you for reading through *Unveiling the Truth* twice with me page by page. Thank you for your endless helpful suggestions and fabulous insight. Thank you for always focusing on and emphasizing what I was doing right, for believing in me, and for being an excellent teacher.

To my fellow memoir class students, thank you for your deep insight and support. Thank you for holding me in strong, solid support, for your awesome suggestions and for writing together.

Thank you to Elissa Altman and her life-changing book, *Permission,* which carried me through some of my darkest hours when I was struggling with the decision of whether I should publish this book. I think your book should be required reading for anyone who writes a memoir. Thank you for helping me to have the strength and courage to persevere with my writing and ultimately to publish and put my work out into the world.

Thank you to Dani Shapiro and her incredible podcast interviewing memoir writers, *Family Secrets.* Your interviews are inspirational and helped give me the courage to write my own memoir.

Thank you to my editor, Dana Chandler, who has helped me through many iterations of this book and guided me through the self-publishing process. I appreciate your excellent work.

Thank you to Sierra Arts who assisted in formatting this book in print and epub format.

And last, but certainly not least, I want to thank my mother, Marilyn Probe, who allowed me to show another perspective by writing her own memoir *Fractured, I Grow Stronger* and gave me permission from beyond the grave to share it. And a special thank you to my brother for sending it to me.

I also want to acknowledge some of the many professionals who helped me heal from my childhood trauma:

Paul Tamminen, my therapist, thank you for being there for me when the memories came back, for using the fabulous technique of EMDR to uncover what happened, and for your constant support and encouragement for me and my whole family.

Kat Lilith, my energy worker, thank you for holding the space for my healing work and giving me priceless insight into how to heal. Thank you for your intuitive readings, encouraging me to laugh and teaching me heart math and other tools to regulate my nervous system. Working with you has helped me to develop my own intuition and have better contact with my higher self. You are my biggest cheerleader, and it means the world to me.

Jen Mann and Karden Rabin, authors of *The Secret Language of the Body* and creators of the online course HEAL, thank you for giving me tools to help retrain my nervous system and allowing me to live my life with more ease and joy.

Anne McInerney, mentor in the HEAL course, thank you for your excellent work one on one with me that targeted the right issues to work on and guided me in the right direction. Thank you for holding space for me to do powerful, transformational healing work.

Isa Metcalf, healer, thank you for your work with quantum healing hypnosis technique (QHHT) and for your help with my chronic pain.

Melissa Griffin, healer, thank you for showing me that spiritual, emotional, and physical healing are inexplicably intertwined. Thank you for helping me unwind and heal the story held in my body.

Note From the Author

Thank you so much for reading! Your support means the world to me. You can help other readers discover this book by leaving a review on Amazon and Goodreads. Every review matters!

Resources and Further Reading

- Altman, Elissa. *Permission: The New Memoirist and the Courage to Create.* Boston: Godine, 2025.
- Beattie, Melody. *Make Miracles in Forty Days: Turning What You Have Into What You Want*. New York: Simon and Schuster, 2010.
- Beck, Martha. *Leaving the Saints: How I Lost the Mormons and Found My Faith*. New York: Crown, 2005.
- Brach, Tara. *True Refuge: Finding Peace and Freedom in Your Own Awakened Heart*. New York: Bantam, 2013.
- Brach, Tara. *Radical Acceptance: Embracing your Life with the Heart of a Buddha*. New York: Random House, 2004.
- Brown, Michael. *The Presence Process: A Healing Journey into Present Moment Awareness*. New York: Beaufort, 2005.

- Chodron, Pema. *When Things Fall Apart: Heart Advice for Difficult Times*. Boston: Shambala, 1996.

- Dechar, Lorie Eve. *Five Spirits: Alchemical Acupuncture for Psychological and Spiritual Healing*. Woodstock, NY: Lantern Books, 2006.

- Dispenza, Joe. *Break the Habit of Being Yourself: How to Lose Your Mind and Create a New One.* New York: Hay House, 2012.

- Dwoskin, Hale. *The Sedona Method: Your Key to Lasting Happiness, Success, Peace and Emotional Well-Being*. Sedona, AZ: Sedona Press, 2003.

- Egoscue, Peter. *Pain Free: A Revolutionary Method for Stopping Chronic Pain*. New York: Bantam, 1998.

- Elizabeth Smart Foundation. Their mission is to drive social change in the face of sexual violence. They provide financial support for survivors. Smart Talk is a podcast where experts and survivors are interviewed.
  https://www.elizabethsmartfoundation.org

- Foo, Stephanie. *What My Bones Know: A Memoir of Healing from Complex Trauma*. New York: Ballantine Books, 2022.

- Gach, Michael Reed. *Acupressure's Potent Points: A Guide to Self-Care for Common Ailments*. New York: Bantam, 1990.

- Gordon, Alan and Alon Ziv. *The Way Out: A Revolutionary, Scientifically Proven Approach to Heal Chronic Pain*. New York: Avery, 2021.

- Goyette, Sue. *The True Names of Birds*. Picton, ON, Canada: Brick Books, 1998.

- Griffin, Melissa. Intuitive Therapeutic Massage. *https://www.besensiblymoved.com*

- Harris, Nadine Burke. *The Deepest Well: Healing the Long-Term Effects of Childhood Adversity*. Boston: Houghton Mifflin Harcourt, 2018.

- *HEAL* course for healing your nervous system *https://somiainternational.com*

- *HEAL* course mentor Anne McInerney Instagram@whispersof.m.e

- Jahnke, Roger. *The Healer Within: Using Traditional Chinese Techniques to Release Your Body's Own Medicine, Movement, Massage, Meditation, Breathing.* New York: HarperOne, 1997.

- Jane Doe No More. A non-profit empowering survivors of sexual crimes.
  https://www.janedoenomore.org

- Lasater, Judith. *Relax and Renew: Restful Yoga for Stressful Times.* Berkeley, CA: Rodmell Press, 1995.

- Levine, Peter A. *Healing Trauma: A Pioneering Program for Restoring the Wisdom of Your Body*. Boulder, CO: Sounds True, 2008.

- Levine, Peter A. *Waking the Tiger: Healing Trauma: The Innate Capacity to Transform Overwhelming Experiences*. Berkeley, CA: North Atlantic Books, 1997.

- Lilith, Kat. Energy Worker *https://www.the-healing-heart.space*

- Luskin, Frederic. *Forgive for Good: A Proven Prescription for Health and Happiness*. New York: HarperOne, 2003.

- Mann, Jennifer and Karden Rabin. *The Secret Language of the Body: Regulate Your Nervous System, Heal Your Body, Free Your Mind*. New York: HarperOne, 2024.

- McLaren, Karla. *The Language of Emotions: What Your Feelings Are Trying to Tell You: Revised and Updated*. New York: St. Martin's Essentials/Sounds True, 2023.

- McLaren, Karla. *Rebuilding the Garden: Healing the Spiritual Wounds of Childhood Sexual Assault*. Santa Rosa, CA: Laughing Tree Press, 1997.

- Metcalf, Isa. Quantum Healing Hypnosis Technique *https://qhhtmiracle.com*

- Miller, Alice. *Thou Shalt Not Be Aware: Society's Betrayal of the Child.* New York: Farrar, Straus, and Giroux, 1984.

- Nakazawa, Donna Jackson. *Childhood Disrupted: How Your Biography Becomes Your Biology, and How You Can Heal.* New York: Atria Books, 2015.

- National Alliance on Mental Health (NAMI) mental health support, education and advocacy. *https://www.nami.org*

- National Center on Sexual Exploitation. Advocacy, litigation and legislation to end sexual exploitation. *https://endsexualexploitation.org*

- Nelson, Bradley. *The Emotion Code: How to Release Your Trapped Emotions for Abundant Health, Love, and Happiness.* New York: St. Martin's Press, 2019.

- Ortner, Nick. *The Tapping Solution: A Revolutionary System for Stress-Free Living*. Berkeley, CA: Hay House, 2013.

- RAINN National Sexual Abuse Hotline and services for survivors of sexual violence *https://rainn.org*

- Ruiz, Don Miguel. *The Four Agreements: A Practical Guide to Personal Freedom*. San Rafael, CA: Amber-Allen Publishing, 1997.

- Schwartz, Richard. *No Bad Parts: Healing Trauma and Restoring Wholeness with the Internal Family Systems Model.* New York: St. Martin's Essential/Sounds True, 2021.

- Shapiro, Dani. *Inheritance: A Memoir of Genealogy, Paternity and Love.* New York: Knopf, 2019. Podcast: Family Secrets on all podcast platforms.

- Shapiro, Francine. *Getting Past Your Past: Take Control of Your Life With Self-Help Techniques From EMDR Therapy*. New York: Rodale Books, 2013.

- Singer, Michael. *The Untethered Soul: The Journey Beyond Yourself.* Oakland, CA: New Harbinger Publications, 2013.

- Stahl, Stefanie. *The Child in You: The Breakthrough Method for Bringing Out Your Authentic Self.* New York: Penguin Life, 2020.

- Survivors of Incest Anonymous is a 12-step program for survivors of incest.
  https://siawso.org

- Tipping, Colin. *Radical Forgiveness: A Revolutionary Five-Stage Process to: Heal Relationships, Let Go of Anger and Blame, and Find Peace in Any Situation.* New York: St. Martin's Essentials/Sounds True, 2010.

- Van Der Kolk, Bessel. *The Body Keeps the Score: Brain, Mind and Body in the Healing of Trauma.* New York: Penguin Books, 2014.

- Vitale, Joe and Ihaleakala Hew Len. *Zero Limits: The Secret Hawaiian System for Wealth, Health, Peace, and More*. Hoboken, NJ: Wiley and Sons, Inc., 2007.

- We Will Organization. Preventing sexual assault and empowering survivors through education, community growth and survivor support.
  https://www.wewillorg.com

- Weller, Francis. *The Wild Edge of Sorrow: Rituals of Renewal and the Sacred Work of Grief*. Berkeley, CA: North Atlantic Books, 2015.

- Wolynn, Mark. *It Didn't Start With You: How Inherited Family Trauma Shapes Who We Are and How to End the Cycle*. New York: Penguin Life, 2016.

- Wu, Baolin. *Qigong for Total Wellness: Increase Your Energy, Vitality, and Longevity with the Ancient 9 Palaces System from the White Cloud Monastery*. New York: St. Martin's Griffin, 2006.

www.ingramcontent.com/pod-product-compliance
Lightning Source LLC
LaVergne TN
LVHW050630100826
845148LV00011B/1814

* 9 7 9 8 2 3 4 0 4 0 2 1 3 *